Praise for *T*  ***racy,***
this book's

"Approach ook us
three years to issues
distilled so expertly in this little on.
– Jeff Orlowski, Director of *The Social Dilemma*

"The issues with internet platforms are well known, but few of us understand the details. In The Little Black Book of Data and Democracy, Kyle Taylor tells us what we need to know and what we can do about it. Everyone should read this book!"
– Roger McNamee, author of the *New York Times* best seller *Zucked: Waking Up to the Facebook Catastrophe*

"A short and practical guide on the shocking truth of how our personal data is being used to undermine democracy."
– Carole Cadwalladr, *Guardian* & *Observer* Journalist, 2018 Orwell Prize Winner & 2019 Pulitzer Prize Finalist

"The Little Black Book of Data and Democracy is, at once, a uniquely accessible primer on how Big Tech functions, a sophisticated analysis of how surveillance capitalism is eroding our consensus reality, and a rousing call-to-action. Kyle Taylor has done a tremendous service by demystifying this existential threat to democracy and offering a roadmap for progress at both the personal and societal level."
– Jesse Lehrich, Co-founder of Accountable Tech and former foreign policy spokesperson for Hillary Clinton

"This is a great, concise primer on how big tech is using our data to poison our societies and imperil our democracies. Even better, the Black Book shows us what we can do to fight back."
– Dr. Heidi Beirich, co-founder of the Global Project Against Hate and Extremism and former director of the Intelligence Project, Southern Poverty Law Center.

"Do you want to be a product or a user? Next to teaching how broken our internet is, this book also empowers us with practical tools and actions to minimise our digital fingerprints. It gears us to resist online manipulation and build awareness in our societies. Get inspired"
– Mikko Salo, Founder of Faktabaari (FactBar), pioneering Finnish digital information literacy and fact-checking service.

"Fresh, engaging and absolutely essential reading for anyone wondering how we piece society back together".
– Katharina Gellein Viken, director – People You May Know

"If you've read the stories about social media and elections over the last several years and found it all a bit overwhelming, this book offers a great entry point to how big data is impacting our society, and what we can do to safeguard democracy."
– Stephen Kinnock MP

"This is a brilliantly readable book about how social media companies have taken our data without asking, fuelled the epidemic of 'fake news' and 'alternative facts', and undermined the shared acceptance of what is true which is so essential to democracy. But, importantly, it also shows how as individuals we are not helpless – we can fight back."
   – Caroline Lucas MP

"Scandals over data mining shocked our democracy with Cambridge Analytica, AggregateIQ and others but most of us are only just beginning to understand it. Kyle Taylor is doing all of us a huge favour with his clear outlining of the story so far and a little bit about what you can do to protect yourself. Read this book – then take some action."
   – Deidre Brock MP

"This book will change the way you use the internet overnight. It is the most complete, comprehensive and timely guide to exactly what happens when we go online. Read it, then read it again"
   – Caolan Robertson, Director Byline TV, Infowars
      whistleblower & author

"When I blew the whistle on the Brexit campaign & Conservative government, I was thrust into the public eye with violent ferocity. Taylor played a central role in translating what was a deeply sinister and complex scandal to the everyday person – guiding me closely on how to explain what had happened to people who didn't know the world I knew. Without his guidance & ability to understand and translate complex political systems, the Cambridge Analytica scandal and subsequent Brexit criminality would not have had such massive public impact. His campaigning and his political ferocity was key to the success and extent of our campaign & whistleblowing. We all owe Taylor a lot in this long fight against the tyranny and violence that social media & data has brought to our democratic systems. If we are to make any real change for the better, then we will need the 12 year old girl in Alabama, all the way to the 80 year old man in London to understand data and it's impact on democracy. I wish I had had this little Black book by my side when I blew the whistle. I am excited for millions of people to finally have access to a conversation that has felt inaccessible for so long. Awareness & education about this new world is integral to creating systemic, structural changes for us to protect democracy and ensure the far right do not continue their tirade. Read it. Then gift it to your grandpa, your aunt, your cousin and (if you have them) your children."

– Shahmir Sanni, Vote Leave Whistleblower and
  Democracy Activist

First Edition

THE LITTLE BLACK BOOK OF SOCIAL MEDIA

—

From innocent tweeting to an attempted coup, how big tech broke democracy – and what you can do about it.

Kyle Taylor

With:

Foreword by Damian Collins MP

LONDON, UNITED KINGDOM

Byline Books

London, United Kingdom

First published in the United Kingdom of Great Britain
and Northern Ireland by Byline Books, 2023

Cover design by Steve Leard

Layout by Prepare to Publish

Printed in Great Britain by Short Run Press Ltd

ISBN UK: 978-1-8384629-8-7

For my parents, who are wonderful

CONTENTS

—

SECTION THREE: WHY IT'S BAD

SECTION FOUR: WHAT YOU CAN DO ABOUT IT

FOREWORD

——

In March 2018, when the story of Cambridge Analytica's use of data harvested from Facebook to micro-target people with political adverts, came to public attention, few had previously commented much on the impact of data on democracy. We tended to see 'fake news' as a content problem, something the social media companies should avoid recommending to users, and when clearly harmful, make sure it was taken down altogether. Even when it was discovered that a Russian state agency had targeted American voters on Facebook with adverts directed from St Petersburg, the immediate focus was on creating greater transparency, rather than understanding the data trail that had made it possible for those campaigns to be launched so effectively.

In March 2021, after a year of QAnon conspiracy theories relating to the 2020 US Presidential election, an attempted insurrection in Washington DC, and conspiracy theories about the coronavirus influencing whether or not people will trust the vaccine that will keep them safe, we understand better the importance of data to the news we see, and the decisions we take.

Democracy rests on shared respect for public institutions and common acceptance of the ties that bring us together. Data has driven the personalisation of news, and the radicalisation of speech within echo chambers where people share the same prejudices and beliefs. The effect of this has been to create more divided societies, and to undermine public trust in politics, government and the news media. This book is a timely reminder of how we got here, and an essential guide to what needs to be done to safeguard democracy in a world driven by data.

Damian Collins MP

March 2021, London

PREFACE: I ONCE THOUGHT THIS WAS A GOOD THING

—

We'd been sitting in the lounge at a house party for 40 minutes. "Come upstairs. We need to talk privately," Chris Wylie had said to me. It was November 2017 and, five months later, Chris would publicly blow the whistle on how Cambridge Analytica had taken the personal Facebook data of over 50 million people without their consent.[1] A week later, Shahmir Sanni would blow the whistle on how Vote Leave – the official campaign for Brexit in the UK – had broken election law in their disinformation-filled quest to take the UK out of the European Union.[2]

Chris and I had known each other for nearly six years, as we were both in the same small circle of progressive UK political activists and campaigners. On this cold winter evening, I thought he wanted to catch up in general as we hadn't seen each other in years. Instead, I suddenly found myself being told in vivid detail about one of the greatest data scandals of all time. We agreed that night his going public had to do more than tell a story – it had to be the catalyst for change. While he focused on laying the story out in the media, I would work on building the campaigning infrastructure necessary to bring about meaningful change.

As the story unfolded in the media, and at risk of retribution, I published online a selection of the actual documents so the public could see for themselves how the law was broken and could support continued lobbying for genuine reform. However, despite the efforts of the campaigners, whistleblowers, journalists and lawyers, three years on almost no new laws have been passed to safeguard elections and protect our democracies.

In 2016 I was working on a coordinated campaign in the US state of North Carolina during the Presidential Election. I was hoping to stop Donald Trump and help elect the first woman to America's highest office. I had run two UK general election constituency campaigns in 2010 and 2015 and would go on to run two more after the US President Election – in 2017 and 2019.

I've worked in and studied campaigns and politics for nearly twenty years. From big-picture strategy to helping to validate the first "big data" model in the UK. Politics was – and still is – my passion. I live and breathe its intensity, its possibility, and its importance. On a single day every so many years, citizens in countries around the world have the opportunity to determine the future of their nation. It's a right not afforded to every human and I've never taken it lightly.

I was at first hugely welcoming of the data revolution in politics. I saw it as an opportunity to understand people better so we could – as campaigners – talk to them about what *they* cared about. A tool that could get more people invested in their future, the future of their country and, quite frankly, the future of the human species. I believed access to more information could only be a good thing. I was wrong.

The foundation was laid by the failings of hyper-capitalism that has left an entire generation poorer than their parents. It was built by people corrupted by power and fueled by business models that are incentivized by division and discord. Access to more information – made possible by technology and so-called "social" media – has, in less than a decade, shifted the planet from a world existing in one shared reality to one that can't even agree on the most basic truths. Feelings are conflated with facts. Facts can now be "alternative." Whatever you "like" is true. Whatever you don't like is "fake news." The technologies that were meant to bring the world together have instead driven us deep into echo chambers where all we want to do – and all we can seem to handle – is to confirm and reconfirm what we *wish* was true, regardless of whether it is or not. All with dire consequences for our mental health and wider society.

Over the following pages I break down – in normal, everyday language with anecdotes and examples – how we got here and what we can do about it. Thanks to brave individuals like Chris Wylie, who blew the whistle on Cambridge Analytica and Facebook, Shahmir Sanni, who blew the whistle on Vote Leave, and Carole Cadwalladr, who started holding power to account years ago and hasn't stopped, we know the truth. Now it's up to us to act on it.

INTRODUCTION: WHAT JUST HAPPENED?

—

Unless you were living under a rock, you probably caught that there was a fairly insane US Presidential Election in 2020. It was arguably the most important election in US history and a significant democratic event for the entire world. Its significance extended far beyond the obvious areas of global security, climate change and response to the global pandemic. The United States – one of the wealthiest countries in the world – responded more poorly to the impact of COVID-19 than almost every country on the planet.

At the heart of the chaos was the role of social media in fueling conspiracy theories about things like mask-wearing, enabling dangerous anti-vaxxers to build a global support base that endangers the very future of humanity. All this COVID-related attention on the harm caused by Facebook in the United States led to grand promises[3] about how it was going to safeguard the election and ensure that their platforms were not used to delegitimise the outcome of the result itself. This of course did not happen. Even after Joe Biden had clearly and fairly been declared the President-Elect, Facebook continued to allow Donald

Trump – and almost anyone for that matter – to post false information about voter fraud and the Election results, doing no more than add a small label under the message[4] itself that the information might be disputed. Users could still like, share and comment on most of the posts. The company admitted internally that they knew the labels were ineffective[5] and yet congratulated themselves publicly[6] for how well they had done at the election.

Over the course of several months from Election Day to Inauguration Day, social media companies continued to allow outright lies about the validity of the election outcome to fester on their services.[7] It didn't help that more than 100 Republicans in the United States House of Representatives and Senate encouraged, enabled and amplified this narrative.[8]

Then, on January 6th, 2021, shortly after 2pm, the unthinkable happened. A group of largely white nationalist, violent insurrectionists breached the walls of the United States Capitol Building in an attempt to disrupt the proceedings to certify Joe Biden as President of the United States and murder democratically elected lawmakers, all with the hope of re-instating Donald Trump as president. The terrorist attack would last for almost seven hours and lead to the deaths of several people.[9]

Social media played a crucial role on the day, with Donald Trump primarily using a public rally and his

Twitter account to instigate, incite then encourage his supporters in their attempts to overthrow the Government.[10] His army of supporters had been driven into an echo chamber where reality was no longer defined by objective truth but instead by what they wished to be true. It was Facebook that served to facilitate the indoctrination, planning and organising of those who committed treason on that day.

Less than a week after the insurrection, Facebook's Chief Operating Officer, Sheryl Sandberg, said in a televised interview, "I think these events were largely organised on platforms that don't have our abilities to stop hate, don't have our standards and don't have our transparency," instead pinning blame on smaller, far-right-enabling platforms including Gab and Parler.[11] She said this despite evidence already existing that showed more than 100,000 Facebook users had posted using the hashtags #FightForTrump and #StopTheSteal, the latter associated with a much wider social media movement built on false claims that the 2020 election was "stolen" by Joe Biden.[12] The original Facebook "Stop The Steal" group was left up for several days immediately following the election in November 2020, racking up more than 300,000 members.[13]

In February 2021, the Program on Extremism at George Washington University pulled together 223 charging documents, which outlined the criminal charges against those arrested in relation to the insurrection. Nearly one-third of them – 73 – made reference to

Facebook and another 20 made reference to Instagram, which is owned by the same parent company, Meta.[14] More than a dozen included live-streamed videos of people saying they intended to attend the riots, with some live-streaming the riots themselves, confirming without question that Facebook played a significant role in facilitating the near-overthrow of a democratically-elected government.[15]

Almost two years later to the day, social media played an almost identical role in Brazil, where supporters of far-right former President Jair Bolsonaro attempted to overthrow the democratically-elected leader of Brazil. Fraud claims were circulating on TikTok and YouTube for nearly a week ahead of the insurrection. Facebook and Twitter were used to coordinate activity on the day, with organisers coding their language to avoid being caught by content moderators.[16] This served to highlight once more how little these companies have done despite serious evidence that they facilitate acts of terror.

Social media's real-world consequences are not limited to elections. When an unarmed black man – Jacob Blake – was shot seven times in the back by police and Black Lives Matter organised protests in Kenosha, Wisconsin, a local militia used Facebook to organise a violent response to the protesters that led to the murder of two people.[17] Mark Zuckerberg, CEO and majority owner of Facebook, described the company's failure to act as an "operational mistake".[18]

Social media's real-world consequences are equally not limited to the United States. Beginning in 2017, the Rohingya Muslim minority in Myanmar became a government-sanctioned target of genocide and to date, more than 900,000 Rohingya have been displaced from their homes.[19] United Nations investigators, while on a fact-finding mission in the area, suggested that Facebook had enabled the rapid spread of hate speech and disinformation that played a "determining role", noting that "everything is done through Facebook in Myanmar...social media is Facebook, and Facebook is social media".[20]

An early publisher of hate speech on Facebook that many believe fueled the ethnic cleansing was Ashin Wirathu, an ultranationalist Buddhist monk who, despite having *been banned by the Myanmar government from preaching publicly*, was allowed to continue spreading false and harmful information on Facebook.[21] The company did not ban him from its platform until months *after* the genocide started.[22] Nearly a year later, Facebook conceded that the company was "too slow" in addressing harmful content in Myanmar, admitting they had only two Burmese-language content moderators against some 30 million Burmese-language users.[23]

In the autumn of 2021, a former Facebook employee, Frances Haugen, became a whistleblower, releasing a trove of internal documents detailing what Facebook knew was occurring on its platform versus what it said publicly. The whistleblower documents included, among other things, an omission that the company "only takes action against approximately 2% of hate speech on the platform" with evidence outlining how internal studies dating back to as early as 2012 showed their algorithmic augmentation (the way of content delivery could lead to offline, real-world harm.[24] In other words, the company's executives had known for *10 years* that their product was a threat to public safety. This isn't simply negligence. It's intentional.

The first half of 2022 felt slightly quieter in the world of social media and then Elon Musk went and bought Twitter. We then spent several months watching a psychodrama play out while the world's once richest man proved every point big tech accountability experts and campaigners had been making for the better part of a decade.

While Mark Zuckerberg controls 57% of voting shares in his company and can unilaterally make all decisions,[25] the situation is even more extreme at Twitter where Elon Musk is the outright private owner of the company. This is thanks, in part, to money from a Saudi Arabian prince and the sovereign wealth fund of Qatar, a country not particularly known for respecting free expression.[26] He then proceeded to fire half of the 7,500 global employees including *the entire* human rights team and accessibility team (which ensures that people of all abilities can use the platform) as well as most of the communications team.[27] The latter made for a very weird few weeks when there was almost nobody at Twitter to comment *about Twitter*.

Musk went on to sack three people who criticised him on social media,[28] further proving his fierce defense of free speech only applies to those saying what he finds acceptable. This was followed by announcing that Twitter would allow back onto the platform all suspended accounts that hadn't broken the law or shared spam. That grouping somehow included Donald Trump, who had used the platform to *incite an insurrection.*[29] The US Congressional January 6th Committee has said Trump was a 'central cause' of the insurrection and made several criminal referrals to the Department of Justice.[30]

The impact has been nothing short of horrifying. Researchers have described the rise in hate speech as "unprecedented," particularly regarding anti-semitic speech, which was up 61% in the first two weeks after Musk's takeover.[31] The soap opera doesn't stop there. Next, he banned several journalists, including those from the *New York Times* and the *Washington Post*, for reporting on his removal of an account that tracked his private jet[32] despite publicly saying he would not ban the jet-tracking account.[33] This led to global condemnation, including from the United Nations.[34] All that in just a few short months, culminating in Musk conducting a poll *on Twitter* asking whether he should step down as CEO. 57.5% of the 17 million people who voted said he should resign.[35] It's almost as if one man having total control over some of the world's most critical communication infrastructure is *not great*.

The ground, of course, was laid over the last two decades as big tech companies ingratiated themselves with the political class and managed to convince the public that their for-profit businesses were somehow different from any other businesses aimed at maximising profit. Now, with so much political and market influence, it's difficult to see how we can take back control of our digital world. Events of recent years have led many to believe that the major tech companies are too big to fix. For the sake of humanity that answer is, quite simply, not acceptable. The first thing we must do is fully understand the problem and start laying out practical solutions. I hope this handbook helps you do just that.

HOW IT ALL WORKS

UNSOCIAL MEDIA

Did you hear? Hillary Clinton is running a child sex trafficking ring from the basement of a pizza place. Except she isn't. The pizza place doesn't even have a basement. And also, of course she isn't.

That didn't stop several news networks from covering the conspiracy and it spread like wildfire on social media, with more than 500,000 posts on Facebook alone in the first week of December 2016, which is when the conspiracy first reached the online mainstream.[36] It even got its own scandal name – Pizzagate! On the surface you could say it's harmless for such nonsensical conspiracy theories to bop around the internet but at the time of the 2016 presidential election, nearly 50% of Trump voters either believed the conspiracy was true or were unsure.[37] It even led to one man driving all night from South Carolina to the pizza place in Washington, D.C. to "free the children." He fired an AR-15 assault weapon three times in the restaurant, likely confused when he discovered there were no children. Or basement.[38]

Studies have shown that "fake news" is more likely to be shared *and* travels six times faster than accurate factual information on social media.[39] That's because conspiracy theories are grounded in feelings, not facts. They drive an emotional response and reinforce something a person already believes, regardless of whether it's true or not.. One conspiracy quickly evolves into another then merges with several others. Pizzagate formed the foundation for QAnon, the most aggressive – and most worrying – modern conspiracy theory. QAnon followers believe a liberal satanist cabal led by people like Hillary Clinton (naturally) are running a global paedophile ring and Donald Trump is going to "free the children." Two QAnon followers were recently elected to the House of Representatives, despite the FBI describing QAnon as bearing the hallmarks of a terrorist organisation.[40] The movement has become a catch-all for pretty much every big conspiracy du jour, including anti-maskers and anti-vaxxers. If you believe one of these conspiracies, you're likely to believe more.[41]

These are just some of thousands of conspiracy theories that slowly made their way through the social media and cable news ecosystem, spurred on by a business model that is great for making Facebook, Twitter, and YouTube (owned by Google) money but terrible for a democratic society.

Why is that? Well, they're all advertising businesses. Facebook makes almost all of its money (98.9%!) from selling ad space on your timeline and selling your data to advertisers.[42] The longer you stay on Facebook, the more ads you'll see. The more ads you see, the more money they make.

So then, what's their main goal? To keep you on Facebook as long as possible so you see as many ads as possible so they make as much money as possible. They do that by collecting as much information on you as possible – called data – so they know what you like and don't like. That way, they can make sure only "stuff you like" appears in your news feed so that you stay longer. Their algorithms – the computer calculation that determines what to show you next – will even try and "nudge" (i.e. manipulate) your online behaviour in order to guide you in certain directions.[43]

By "stuff you like" I mean stuff that makes you feel certain emotions, like happy or – more effectively – angry or fearful.[44] The happy stuff is pretty straightforward and comes from personal posts your "Facebook friends" share. "OMG, we're on a vacay and here's a pic of the pretty beach!" or "We're pregnant! Due in March!" While this stuff is definitely happy, it's also designed to trigger FOMO – fear of missing out – which makes us feel bad about our own lives.[45] The worse we feel, the more we want to buy stuff to make us feel better. "I'm not on vacation. I'm single and I'll never have a baby. Now I'm sad. I'll buy some stuff from the ads to feel better." Sneaky, right?

The angry stuff usually comes from politics. Something a politician or their "side" may have done that gets you all hot and bothered. It's very "us and them" and the more you read, like, share, and click, the more similar – and more extreme – stuff you'll see as they try and keep you on their platform longer and longer. That way you'll click more ads and make them more money. The problem is, lots of this stuff isn't even true because platforms like Facebook, Twitter, and YouTube don't really have any rules that people have to tell the truth when they're exercising "political speech."[46] Unlike other media industries, there is still no real government regulation over these platforms.[47]

Slowly over time, after you've seen the same stuff again and again, you might start to believe it's true. Like that Hillary Clinton is running a child sex ring from the basement of a pizza place that doesn't even have a basement. Meanwhile, someone else – who has been sent down a totally different but equally extreme rabbit hole of stuff on their Facebook feed or YouTube playlist will be living in a completely alternate reality. Over time, it starts to feel like we're existing in different worlds. That's when democractic society starts to totally break down. Like right now.

This is all because Facebook's business model – the way they make money – benefits from it. After all, they aren't a public body or a charity. They're a private business trying to make as much money as possible. The whole setup may be good for them, but it's bad for democracy.

When you realise and accept that as true, then you actually start to make sense of why Facebook has upended our world and acknowledge that maybe it's not all that harmless.

Over the next few short chapters I'm going to do my best to briefly and clearly explain how the current situation came about, what it's doing to us and what we can do about it. I won't cover everything because this is meant to be an easily understandable introduction (please don't Tweet @ me pointing out all the stuff I didn't say). Sit back, relax and get ready to have your mind blown, like when you found out Hillary Clinton is running a child sex ring from the basement of a pizza place in Washington, D.C. (she isn't).

THE EVOLUTION
OF TARGETING

—

"Targeting" is the practice of finding the right incentive – the message – to get someone to do something. Nike wants you to buy their shoes. Apple, their i-things. In politics, politicians want you to vote for them. Long gone are the days of making your case as to how your things – shoes, gadgets or candidates – are better than the other things. Now it's all about feelings and emotions. Nike is selling inspiration. Apple is selling "cool." Politicians are selling hope and, more regularly, fear.

This practice isn't new but it's certainly more sophisticated now. I'm not going to go back to Roman times or something but we can look to the late 1950s to really get a handle on this. February 18th, 1959 to be precise. That's the day The Simulmatics Corporation said "hey, we're open!" They believed even then that if they got enough information about people, they could predict how people would act using super simple early computing. Namely, how they'd vote. It was BASIC then. Think generally like "you shouldn't talk about civil rights in the South," not super specific like "Bob on Smith Street supports marriage equality." This type of intel was cutting edge at the time and it likely helped John F. Kennedy win the 1960 US Presidential election.[48]

Now let's fast forward to the 1990s because that's when this gets way more interesting. Remember magazines? For those younger readers out there, they're big glossy printed things that used to be placed by checkout counters in supermarkets. With titles like "Auto Week" and "Horse and Hound", they were aimed at people's more specific interests and they were hugely popular.[49] Political strategists started to realise that you can tell a lot about a person based on which magazines they read. They started using this subscription data to target messages (remember: these are incentives to get people to do something) that would resonate with particular people with the hope that it would make said people vote for their candidate.

In politics it's all about telling voters specific stuff about politicians that you think will get them to vote how you want them to vote. It can be favourable about your candidate or unfavourable about your opponent. For example, let's say someone subscribes to "Vegetarian Monthly". You can probably guess that they're, you know, a vegetarian. Which means they probably care about animal rights. So you can send them stuff – at the time, *postcards in the mail* – about how your candidate LOVES animals or how your opponent eats tons of meat. Maybe even a picture of the opponent shoving a piece of steak in their mouth. This probably doesn't seem very sophisticated now, but back then it was a game-changer.

As computers got smarter, data got easier to store and manipulate. Suddenly, more things you did were "insights" into who you were and what you cared about.

The next big leap in data analytics was supermarket "club cards." From Wegman's "Shopper Club" in the USA to Sainsbury's "Nectar Points" in the UK, you'll be shocked to learn the primary purpose of them *isn't* to give you discounts when you buy your 37th packet of chicken tenders. The real aim is to build a massive database of all the things you buy and how often you buy them. Many supermarkets then sell this data to other companies, who use it to build a profile of you.[50] Buy dog food regularly and live in a city? You probably have a pet and rely on parks for walks. That means you care about green spaces and I can target a message to you about that. Never buy meat? That means you're probably a vegetarian. You may even subscribe to "Vegetarian Monthly."

This was revolutionary in the late 2000s. Most people have to go to the supermarket often because we all have to, you know, eat. And we buy lots of stuff at the supermarket. If you think about "big box" retail like Target in the USA (they've got the Target Circle) to Tesco Superstores in the UK ("Scan your Tesco

ClubCard to get ClubCard points!"), you can add in cleaning supplies, clothes, housewares and those ski poles on offer at the end of the aisle that you really don't need because you don't even know how to ski "but they're only £9 so chuck them in the cart!"

The data from different stores – usually legal to buy and sell thanks to those terms and conditions you probably didn't read – were combined into a "cocktail" to give a snapshot of a voter. Many political parties would use the 300-400 data points to build a profile of a person and give the person a score of how likely they were to vote for the political party and for their opponents. For people the political party didn't have data for, they could "match" them based on geography or type of housing or something they *did* know to make an educated guess as to how they might also vote. Suddenly, you knew where your likely supporters lived and you hadn't even talked to them yet.

Next, you'd have a few thousand real conversations with people to confirm whether your predictions were correct and if they were, then away you'd go. It saved time (you didn't have to bother talking to people who would definitely support you or those who definitely wouldn't) and by extension, money. This was the first sign of bad times to come because it suddenly prioritized a smaller subset of the population – the votes that were "up for grabs" – and excluded the vast majority of people. We call this a "democractic deficit" because if you don't engage people in democracy, they lose interest. The more interest they lose, the less their voice is heard. That's bad for society. Is it any wonder voter turnout began to collapse in the early 2000s and didn't rebound until the recent resurgence of right-wing populism?

Even this lower level of data-driven politics was starting to cause a breakdown in democracy. The world really wasn't ready for what came next in the form of Facebook, which proudly claims to have 52,000 data points on you. These data points – from the shape of your chin (face recognition) to what you read (newspaper articles shared), they've built a profile of you that's so complex, some claim they can predict what you'll do even better than you can.[51] But first, a quick word on barn animals.

THE VIRTUAL COW GOES "MOO MOO GIVE ME ALL YOUR DATA"

Remember FarmVille? It was that highly addictive, all-consuming Facebook game where you'd have to set up and manage a fake digital farm. "Bob invited you to play FarmVille." "Susan invited you to play FarmVille." "Karen invited you to play FarmVille." If you were on Facebook anytime from 2009 to 2011, you probably remember these notifications because they were CONSTANT. And they worked. By the end of 2009 – the same year FarmVille launched – the game had 60 million users.[52] Its usage peaked in 2010, when it boasted over 80 million regular monthly users.[53] Why am I mentioning it now, do you ask? Because it's where casually giving up all your data really began.

It used the principles of gambling to get people to buy fake "farm cash" with real money so they could buy fake stuff (remember, a tractor in a virtual farm isn't real).[54] The more troubling and lasting impact of FarmVille is how it normalized the idea of clicking "accept" to complex, invasive terms and conditions that legitimized the handover of large amounts of our personal data without really explaining the impact. Buried in their 2010 terms and conditions was the following:

"We may offer you the opportunity to submit other information about yourself (such as gender, age, occupation, hobbies, interests, zip code, etc.), or we may be able to collect that information from social networking systems on which you have used Zynga Games or SNS [social networking] Apps (in accordance with the terms of use of those systems)."[55]

Signing up also gave Zynga – the developer of the game – access to your friend list and their public profile (which is why you got all those annoying notifications). Think about that for a second – a seemingly harmless game where you make a fake farm *needs* permission to access all your friend information and their public profile data. Zynga could access it from Facebook *without* getting permission from your friends because Facebook's terms and conditions – which I'm sure you also didn't read – allowed them to do that. So now they know who you're connected to and – by analysing all those public profiles – can figure out *why* you're all connected based on what you have in common. From mutual friends to where you live, your favourite movies and what Facebook pages – including news sources – you read, they're building a profile of not just you but your entire network. All because you wanted to feed some fake cows some fake food. Once people had been eased into giving up their data selves for nothing, the landscape was ripe for moving beyond games into the world of politics.

CAMBRIDGE ANALYTICA 101

In the new world of digital political campaigning, consulting firms started popping up left, right and far-right. They promised political campaigns incredible insights based on the models they were building for individual voters. The most notorious of these firms was Cambridge Analytica. With a massive investment from Robert Mercer and the backing of Trump's right-hand man Steve Bannon, the firm worked on campaigns around the world in support of dictators, despots and – wait for it – Donald Trump.[56]

You're probably looking at that fancy schmancy name and thinking "wow, that sounds fancy schmancy!" It's not. Chris Wylie told me the "Cambridge" was put there to sound impressive (associating it with Cambridge in the UK) and the "Analytica" is just a made up word, aimed at sounding – yes, you guessed it – fancy schmancy.

Their aim was to co-opt military psychological warfare tactics developed by the US military and turn these information weapons on the voting public. Their method was built on what's called psychographics, which is yet another fancy schmancy word that just means studying people based on their interests, activities and feelings.[57] Let's take a look at that through the lens of a dating profile.

You're probably familiar with demographics, which are facts about people. I'm 36. I make $35,000 a year. I live in London. I identify as male and I'm single. Psychographics are more personal. I enjoy slow walks through the forest. I like pop music and I love cheeseburgers (sorry readers of "Vegetarian Monthly"). They're way more revealing.

Cambridge Analytica built their profiles of people using what's called the "OCEAN" model, giving people scores on Openness (Are you up for new things?), Conscientiousness (Are you a thoughtful friend?), Extroversion (Do you like the spotlight?), Agreeableness (Are you kind?) and Neuroticism (Are you anxious a lot?).[58] Manipulating these beneath-the-surface traits about you makes for way more effective advertising, whether it's shoes or, say, a candidate for President of the United States. Often, the core emotion you want to make people feel is fear.

For example, if you're running for President on a platform of "law and order", you can target people who "like" the police or the military on Facebook. Or you can target people who live in suburbs and rarely experience crime (which is likely since crime has been consistently dropping in the USA, UK and most developed countries for the past thirty years)[59] with looped videos of extreme examples of crime in far-off places. This will make them feel deep, deep fear that isn't based in reality but nevertheless elicits an extreme fear response and gets people to do what you want: vote for your candidate.

First though, you need lots of data on people so you know how to push their buttons. Cambridge Analytica had that data because they took it from people without their permission. They worked with a researcher in Cambridge, England named Dr. Alexander Kogan (who at one point referred to himself professionally as Dr. Spectre… like the Bond villain) who developed a seemingly harmless Facebook app called "thisisyour-digitallife" that seemed like a quiz from a 1998 Teen Vogue magazine.[60] 270,000 people took it.[61]

When each of those 270,000 people played the quiz, the app also took the Facebook profile information of ALL of their Facebook friends without those friends' permission, which gave Dr. Spectre – apologies, Dr. Kogan – and in turn Cambridge Analytica, who he then worked with – the data of around 50 million Facebook users.[62] Again, without consent. In short, they *stole the personal data of nearly 50 million people* (including my data after my Facebook friend used the app).

Then Cambridge Analytica went and worked first for Ted Cruz then for Donald Trump with all that data, targeting Facebook ads at people who had no idea Cambridge Analytica used all their data to conduct psychological warfare against millions of Americans.

You might be thinking: "So what? I've got nothing to hide and I make my own decisions! Nothing influences me!" That's not the point and it's also not true, but we'll come to that later. Stealing data isn't like stealing a car. The stolen car moves from place A to place B. You either find it or you don't; but either way it's only one car in one place at one time. Data is easily transferable. It's easily duplicated. And it's almost impossible to trace. If your data was stolen like mine was, you have no way of knowing where it is, how many times it was copied, who it was sold to or what it's being used for.

IF YOU'RE NOT PAYING FOR THE PRODUCT, YOU <u>ARE</u> THE PRODUCT

Nothing is free. When you're not paying for something with money, you can be sure it's costing you in different ways. One of those ways is by turning you into the product. This is particularly true with many tech companies and especially true when it comes to social media companies like Facebook, Twitter and Google.

You'll be familiar with the traditional "relationship" you've had with a business. They have something you want – a coffee, for example – or a service like your cell phone contract. You give them money and they give you goods or a service. It's a fair transparent exchange.

There are some tech companies that do this. Take Apple, for example. You give them money and they give you an iPhone or iPad or some other iThing. Or, you give them money and they provide a service like Apple Music or AppleTV+ or Apple Something Else. They're almost totally a direct exchange business.

Not Facebook. Or Twitter. Or Google (for the most part). They give you a service like their platform or their search engine but you don't give them any money. Instead, you give them data on you – when you use their products, what you look for, when you look for it, who you know (those pesky Facebook "friends"), where you live, what you eat (all those foodie pics), and on and on and on. They use that data to sell advertising space. Their customers are hundreds of thousands of businesses, charities, governments, political campaigns and individuals who buy space in your news, your search results page, your email inbox, your Instagram feed and on and on and on. The more time you spend and the more things you click (because everything you click tells them something else about you) makes you even more valuable to their actual customers (remember, that's the folks buying ad space).

You'll recall Facebook claims to have up to 52,000 data points on every user. As fabulously interesting as we all are, did you even think there were that many data points about you? They fall into several categories. One is called "DeepText" which is tons of data that can come from commercial data brokers like where you shop and what you buy. A second is called "DeepFace," which is used to identify people in pictures so you can "tag" them (not so innocent, linking a friend in a photo). The third is called "FB Learner Flow" which uses predictive models to try and calculate future decisions you might make based on stuff you've already done to decide which ads to send you IN THE FUTURE.[63] Basically, use your past actions to predict your future needs (to sell ads).

For example, let's say you announce on Facebook you're pregnant. Well, now Facebook can tell its advertisers that you'll be buying a stroller, a car seat, baby clothes and a million other things soon. This helps explain sometimes why you might feel like your phone is listening (it very well may be but we'll get to that later). Still, you don't have to say stuff for it to learn. It's capturing everything you post.

Combine all that data and information about you with all that data and information they're collecting on billions of people and all of a sudden they know more about a majority of people on earth than any other entity on the planet ever has. That's really valuable.

In 2018, each Facebook user in the United States was worth – on average – $111.97 EACH to Facebook.[64] Their total ad revenue in 2019 was over $69 billion.[65] In 2020 that rose to nearly $85 billion and in 2021, a staggering $115 billion.[66] So you're providing them with a good (you) and a service (your time on their platform). Did they pay you anything for that? Yeah, I didn't think so.

You're not their customer. You're what they're selling.

WHAT'S UNDER THE HOOD

NOT-SO-DELICIOUS COOKIES

——

I'm sure you hear the word cookie and you say to yourself "yum, cookies!" The name actually came from fortune cookies, which have an embedded message in them like "your deepest self is already inside you" (I made that up. Not bad, right?).[67] This makes sense because an internet "cookie" is a little piece of information that a website – from Google to Amazon to *The New York Times* – stores on your computer and can later access again. When you visit most websites, information like what you clicked on, what time it is, how long you spent there and where you're located is tracked. It is then stored in your personalised cookie file.[68] The file is created by the website but stored by your computer's browser software – like Chrome, Firefox or Safari.[69] When you revisit the site again at a later date, your computer sends that old information it stored last time you were there right back to the site.

That means the website "knows" that you have been there before and uses all that information it collected on your last visit to customise your experience so it's "just for you." Don't you feel special?! Some cookies (called session cookies) only exist for one visit and are deleted when you close the browser. These are pretty harmless.

But there is also something called a third-party persistent cookie. I know, what a mouthful (pun intended). More commonly called a "tracking" cookie, these can be accessed by websites that didn't even create them! So when you visit a new website somewhere else on the internet that seems totally different, the experience will be customised "just for you". Even though you haven't even been to that website before. These are used by advertisers to target people with products they might like because of their behaviour elsewhere online.[70]

Since you're not paying for the product, you are the product. Everywhere you go on the internet. All the time. These cookies are more like the story of Hansel and Gretel, leaving a trail of little cookie crumbs tracking everywhere you've been online, working to figure out where you might go next. Instead of a wicked witch though, it's just thousands of companies that know pretty much everything about you trying to advertise stuff at you.

Take a moment and visualise the internet like a physical highway where there are lots of billboards everywhere. Unlike a physical highway where the ads have to be for everyone who drives by, on the internet highway every single billboard is designed specifically for you based on how you reacted to all of the other billboards.

In the European Union, there is something called the General Data Protection Regulation which requires websites to ask you if you're cool with cookies (not so in the United States. They don't even have to ask).[71] How they do that, however, isn't consistent and it's WAY HARDER to disable them than it is to just say yes.

For example, take *The Guardian*'s website. I've picked it specifically to make a point. Even the 'left-wing liberal media conspiracy' is doing this, you left-wing liberal reader! When you go to *The Guardian* website, it asks you to opt into cookies and it looks really warm and fuzzy:

It's "my choice" and it's all about making my experience better for me! What's not to like? They're just trying to help me out! This is the most common way stuff that isn't really good for you is framed. If a website is telling you it's about convenience and personalization, they're probably taking your data.

If I'm happy, it's easy! I click "Yes, I'm happy." If I'm not, I have to "manage my cookies." BORING! Note there isn't an easy "No thanks" option. Either yes, or manage.

So I click manage and I get this super complicated, super long set of categories and lists:

I've got purposes and features and site vendors and then I've got sub-categories of "User Content" and "Legitimate Interest." Without a degree in Information Privacy Law how would any normal person know what all of this means?

The option to "Reject all" is now available on the screen but it is in a small font and not very obvious. Some consent purposes are somewhat clear – "store and access information on my computer, personalise ads, ensure security," etc. "Features" is when it starts to get more confusing. They want to "match and combine offline data sources." Huh? If you click the drop-down it says vendors will be allowed to "Combine data obtained offline with data collected online in support of one or more Purposes or Special Purposes", then it lists dozens of vendors who will get to do this. What offline data are they talking about and where did these vendors get that?

Next, I click the tab labeled "Site Vendors" only to discover it is a long scrolling list of over FIVE HUNDRED (I counted them one-by-one) site vendors located all around the world (including Facebook, Google and Amazon), each with a different specific profile. I pick one at random – 360e-com Sp. z o.o, which a Google search tells me is located in Poland – and it's drop down says it wants to select personalised ads, create a personalised ads profile identification and apply market research to generate audience insights, among a raft of other things.

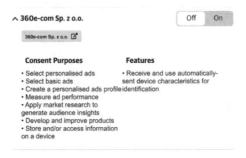

Remember, all of this would have been automatically opted in if I had clicked "Yes, I'm happy." But I wanted to "Manages my preferences" like some sort of dumb-dumb. So I click "reject all" and I'm done with it, but only for this time. Because EVERY TIME I come to *The Guardian*'s website, I'll only be presented with two options "Yes, I'm happy" or "Manage my preferences," where I'll have to go through this process all over again.

I mention this because it gets to the heart of a central problem with any attempt at protecting people's privacy online. The default is almost always to give all your data away and it's the user – YOU – who has to do the work to opt out. Why? Because you're not the customer. You're the product. The internet is just one long highway lined with billboards all owned by tech companies selling advertising space to other companies who want to sell YOU stuff. The default is to give them all the power, not you.[72]

THE INTERNET IS NOT THAT INNOCENT

—

By now you might be thinking: "This book is supposed to be about data and democracy. There's been a lot about data but when do we get to the democracy bit?" Be patient. We'll get there. The book isn't dense so you won't have to wait that long. It's important to fully understand how messed up these companies are at their core.

Let's start with Google search.

93% of all online experiences start with a search engine.[73] Since we say "Google it" and not "Bing it" or DuckDuckGo it" it will come as no surprise to learn that 88% of all searches in the USA[74] and a whopping 92% of all searches in the UK[75] were done on Google. Once people have searched, 75% of the time they don't scroll past the first page of results.[76]

That means that almost all of the time, a person's entire Internet experience is determined by what Google and its algorithm decides to put on the first page of search results. Since they make money from selling ad space, they are financially incentivised to prioritise the highest-paying advertisers and their own products and services. Their interest isn't in offering you the best results for you but the most profitable results for them. Your search is their product, not their service.

Onward now, with my winner for absolute worst and we'll move backwards (or sidewards) from there.

FACEBOOK IS TAKING THE DATA OF PEOPLE WHO AREN'T EVEN ON FACEBOOK

—

Facebook bought WhatsApp for $19 billion and they did it for the same reason Google paid $1.6 billion for the loss-making YouTube: data. Tech giants buy seemingly unprofitable companies to monopolise their access to behavioural data that they can then incorporate into their advertising business model.[77] Interestingly, the European Commission – one branch of the European Union's government – only gave Facebook permission to buy WhatsApp because they received assurances that data flows from the two businesses would remain separate.[78]

Unfortunately – yet predictably – Facebook has since reneged on that assurance. In 2016, the company linked WhatsApp phone numbers with profiles on Facebook.[79] This was challenged in Brussels and eventually led to a €110 million fine, which is basically nothing for a company worth over $500 billion.[80] To put that into context, let's say you make $50,000 a year. That would be like getting fined $13. Yes, THIRTEEN DOLLARS. It's basically nothing.

While WhatsApp messages are indeed "end-to-end" encrypted (meaning not even WhatsApp can view your messages), Facebook can and does collect other sorts of what's called "metadata" from the app: your phone number, your contact list, your personal information, who you message, when you message them, and how often.[81] You know, all that stuff you probably thought was private information. All of this is used to personalise and increase the information Facebook holds about you and then sells to advertisers.[82] Don't just take our word for it, a since deleted FAQ on WhatsApp's own website informed users how to, "choose not to share my account information with Facebook to improve my Facebook ads and products experiences".[83]

This isn't super surprising. Mark Zuckerberg himself, who founded Facebook and serves as its CEO, admitted to the United States Congress that they collect data on non-Facebook users.[84] For example, the "People You May Know" feature that asks you to invite "People You May Know" to Facebook. Ever wonder how Facebook knows "People You May Know"? Facebook is also working on plans to connect the messaging services of Instagram – a public social media platform that it also owns – and WhatsApp.[85] How can you keep the latter encrypted if it's merged with something that's public?

YOUTUBE – OWNED BY GOOGLE – IS A HOT-BED OF RADICALISATION

—

YouTube is perhaps the perfect case study of the way the internet creates echo chambers with what are called 'reconfirming algorithms'. As a reminder, an algorithm is a set of rules that analyses data – like yours – to figure out something, like what video you might watch next, which is surprisingly far more harmful than you might think. In this context, it reconfirms that you might be, for example, someone who believes Hillary Clinton is running a paedophile sex ring from the basement of a pizza place.

In 2006, Google paid $1.65 billion for YouTube, a company that had never made a profit and was inundated in copyright infringement lawsuits.[86] Why? To increase and streamline data harvesting. YouTube was, and still is, massively popular. In the game of data harvesting, how many users you have really matters. Now, all those YouTube users are on a Google platform and Google can track and record their behaviour. But in recent years it has become increasingly clear that YouTube is a radicalising machine.[87]

Soon after Google purchased YouTube, it introduced advertisements on the website. Not long after that, it started giving people who put videos on YouTube a cut of the money companies like Nike were paying to advertise on their videos. The more views you get, the more you are paid. It's sort-of like a pyramid scheme. Google gets YouTubers to use you – the product – to get more advertisers – their actual customers – and gives the content creators a cut. This, of course, incentivises provocative and sensationalistic content because the longer people spend on YouTube, the more money Google can make. The goal is to sell as many ads as possible so Google wants to keep you on the platform as long as possible. Google does that by only showing you stuff you'll definitely like, whether it's cat videos or "lock her up" Hillary Clinton mash-ups.

For example, let's say you're slightly interested in this "Pizzagate" thing you've heard about. So you watch a video made by some random person on YouTube. (Why we're inclined to believe unverified, total strangers on social media when we wouldn't do that in real life is another dangerous phenomenon of the internet age). YouTube's algorithm goes "Hey, you like that? Here's something a bit more extreme about how the Clintons are actually running a global paedophile ring. But first, watch this short ad (cha-ching!). Keep them happy, keep them watching, make more money. Did that draw your attention? Well here's one about ANOTHER conspiracy involving the Clintons. But first, another ad. (cha-ching!))." Before you know it, you're watching clips promoting QAnon, the fringe group mentioned earlier that's organising a global movement to "free the children from a Satanist Liberal Hollywood cult" that doesn't exist. That's the one the FBI – even under the Trump administration – says has the markers of a terrorist organisation.[88]

So someone who's curious about a thing they heard – possibly on Facebook or Twitter – becomes a totally radicalised conspiracy theorist living in an alternate reality that was incentivised by YouTube's business model. Not ideal.

This combination of monetisation and person-alisation has been a boon for radical and fringe ideologies, particularly on the far right. In January 2020, research presented at the ACM Conference on Fairness, Accountability and Transparency in Barcelona confirmed what many had been saying for years: people who watched "moderate" content on YouTube were likely to migrate towards increasingly radical videos.[89] Promoters of extreme rightwing ideology (who evidence suggests are more inclined towards shocking, provocative and emotional-ly-charged content)[90] have exploited YouTube's design to entice larger and larger audiences.[91] And YouTube has allowed this because larger audiences mean more ads sold (cha-ching!). That incentive –

making as much money as possible in an information business – is maybe, kinda (read: TOTALLY) not in the best interest of democracy.

To function, a democracy requires an accurately informed society that lives in a shared reality. As I have explained, this does not exist on the internet. On a platform like YouTube, the highly sophisticated (and secret) algorithm determines what videos appear on your homepage and on your "up next" section. Everyone's YouTube is a highly personalised place. Just log out of your Google account and check: the new YouTube you see will be very different.

AMAZON – YOUR OTHER ROOMMATE

—

As for Amazon, In many ways it might seem different to the other tech giants. After all, it has a recognisably pre-internet business model. "But it is just a shop online," you say. "How could it be bad? I can get everything I need all in one place!" More stuff, more data.

In recent years Amazon has been moving into the world of Google and Facebook-style data harvesting and surveillance.[92] Like these two companies, Amazon sells the extensive data it holds on its users (in this case, their shopping and viewing habits) to advertisers.[93] Amazon's Alexa, however, is taking this practice into new territory. Alexa is an AI voice assistant device that you keep in your home and can speak to; a portal to the internet that can provide information, order you a product, turn on your music and even read you a recipe. Convenient, right? Don't forget what convenient usually means. More data.

Alexa is more than just a device. Amazon has made it very easy for third-party developers (that's other companies that create stuff for Amazon's products) to connect to Alexa. The aim is to build an integrated environment that unifies all "smart" devices in your home, workplace, or wherever else, from lights to the thermostat to your refrigerator.[94] Dave Limp, Alexa's senior vice president, explained the goal as being to, "create a kind of open, neutral ecosystem for Alexa... and make it as pervasive as we possibly can".[95] They don't even pretend they care about your privacy.

With Alexa, Amazon is leading the way in the implementation of online data harvesting practices into the offline world.[96] Amazon claims the device only listens to you when you have activated it with a request, but the company's patent applications in the U.S. show that Amazon is pre-planning how Alexa and connected devices could be used to monitor customers' private behaviour and then nudge them towards personalised advertisements for products.[97] For example, it might hear you talking to your partner about how it has been raining a lot lately and start delivering ads to you across the internet for umbrellas. That may seem innocent enough but what if you're talking about being HIV positive and then start to have trouble getting health insurance? Or you express gratitude that your criminal record was expunged and won't show up on your background check then suddenly have job interviews canceled?

This all-invasive future may already be here as there is mounting evidence that Alexa and devices like it are already listening to you even when they're turned "off".[98]

Also owned by Amazon is the Ring in-home security camera system, which has been sold to "bring protection" to your house. Unless, of course, somebody hacks into the one you've placed in your children's bedroom and begins speaking to them through the built-in speaker while they watch, which happened to a family in Tennessee, USA.[99] Nothing says security like discovering a stranger may have been watching you for days without your knowledge.

"SMART" SPEAKERS AND THAT SUPERCOMPUTER IN YOUR POCKET

Have you had it happen to you that you were talking about something and then you opened Instagram and started getting ads for that thing? Your first thought is "OMG my phone is listening to me." If you tell that thought to your friends, you're often shut down as being "paranoid." You're not paranoid.

The biggest player in the "listening" market is Amazon Echo devices. These devices listen out for that keyword "Alexa" so they can make your life "more convenient" and do something for you. You'll remember that if something is selling convenience, it's likely taking your data and that's as true as ever with Alexa. But to listen out for that word, it has to listen to all your words. Amazon itself admits this is true (again, they aren't even hiding it *so why don't we believe them?*). Amazon claims it is always listening so the artificial intelligence can "learn."[100]

Google got caught up in a bit of a whoopsy daisy when it "accidentally upgraded" enabled auto-listening on some people's devices who hadn't signed up for their "home security" offering. You read that right. Their "home security" offering that you *pay for* keeps the speaker listening all the time so it can hear fire alarms and warn you. It's just helpful, see?[101]

A Berlin-based company even managed to build eight "smart spies" apps that received approval in one form, but were subsequently updated to spy through Amazon Echo and Google Home devices.[102] If this small Berlin-based company can do it, imagine what mega corporations like Amazon and Google themselves can do. Or governments for that matter. Do you really want a private company – or your government – to be able to listen to every word you say?

If you leave your Android device or iPhone on the default settings it came with, everything you say could be recorded and used for marketing purposes not just by the company that made the phone but by third-party apps (that's almost EVERY app) that you install.[103]

This was tested recently. A Vice reporter started saying key words and phrases several times a day for five days. Within 24 hours of starting, he was getting ads for the stuff he'd been saying. He said "back to University" and started getting ads for summer courses. He said "cheap shirts" and started getting ads for – you guessed it – cheap shirts. Some companies deny this while others – like Google – are open about it. But for most, their terms and conditions – and the law – don't prohibit it.[104]

This entire, all-encompassing system of treating information about you as nothing more than a commodity for profit – called surveillance capitalism by Shoshana Zuboff[105] – now extends way beyond advertising. From watches that track your heart rate around the clock to "smart fridges" that know when you're low on milk, every bit of data about you is stored and used with the sole objective of making money, regardless of the human implications.

A PICTURE OF YOU AT 70. WORTH IT?

FaceApp, owned by the Russian developer Wireless Lab, is an app that uses AI to playfully recreate your face, transforming the picture of the user to make them smile or frown, look younger or older. Sounds harmless enough. Until you start to read the smallprint. By using the app, you hand over all rights to the use of your likeness. "Perpetual use", in the words of FaceApp's terms of service, "to use, reproduce, modify, adapt, publish, translate, create derivative works from, distribute, publicly perform and display your user content and any name, username or likeness provided in… all media formats and channels now known or later developed without compensation to you". Basically, "you give us all of this for free and we give you a digital picture of yourself looking old. And you're welcome."[106]

The app doesn't stop there though. It also collects other data stored on your device, such as the websites you visit.[107] At an individual level, the implications of this are severe. Clearly, the risk of identity theft would be high if that sort of data – YOUR FACE – was to fall into the wrong hands.[108]

But the real dangers go much further than that. Numerous tech companies are using facial image and video data to "train" facial recognition algorithms. This technology is already so sophisticated that tiny modules can scan a person's facial points to interpret imperceptible micro-expressions and eye movements, and then recognize from them human emotions, moods and even intentions.[109] Our faces can reveal a lot about us, from whether we are ill to how a bit of information makes us feel – happy, sad, angry and fearful. Remember how important those last two are? A study published by Stanford University in 2017 found that AI could even deduce someone's sexuality just by scanning photos of their face.[110]

The implications and risks of this technology – from law enforcement to politics, business to medicine – are huge. A government or company that has the ability to read from someone's face their sexuality or their "likelihood to commit a crime" (Remember that Tom Cruise film *Minority Report*?), or understand, with minute precision, their preference for a certain product or political party, could consolidate a huge amount of power. They could decide to discriminate against people because an app says they're gay. Or arrest someone because they "fit a description" that includes propensities determined via their data. Or even pre-arrest someone before they commit a crime. This would inevitably further entrench the massive racial disparities that already plague the real world.

A federal study in the USA recently found that Black, Asian and Native American people were up to 100 times more likely to be misidentified by facial recognition systems than white people.[111] 100 times! Not only are these technologies performing poorly, giving them primacy over human decision making is extremely dangerous.

Facial recognition technology poses perhaps the greatest rising threat to people's civil liberties and freedoms. What happens when the burden of proof shifts so the state doesn't have to prove you're guilty but you have to prove your innocence? It could turn the entire justice system on its head, and not in a good way.

THIS IS YOUR BRAIN ON DRUGS. I MEAN SOCIAL MEDIA.

——

Before we go on, let's review. First, we covered the history of big data and advertising. Then we learned about the convoluted business models of big tech companies that incentivize keeping people on the platform to sell as many ads as possible, which drives extreme content that plays on people's emotions. Then we looked under the hood at the mechanics of this stuff. After that, you probably found a nice cosy cupboard to cry in for a few minutes before making a cup of tea to calm your nerves. Trigger warning: it's going to get worse before it gets better because I've got to tell you about how all this stuff plays with – and rewires – how our brains work.

We're living in the "information age." There's tons of information. More than ever. And we consume it constantly. Whether it's that news app you're checking for the twelfth time today, or the hundredth time you log onto Facebook or Instagram or Twitter, or reading this book, we spend more hours than ever putting more information than ever into our brains.

A 2007 study suggested we're exposed to 5,000 ads a day.[112] FIVE THOUSAND. And that was in 2007. Add in our news feeds, our Reddit forums and our podcasts, and that number has likely doubled since then.

This is compounded by the 'infinite scroll'. It's how we describe the fact that the page 'never ends' on social media sites like Facebook, Instagram and Twitter. You can scroll and scroll literally forever and there will always be more information provided to you. In fact, it has the same effect on people as gambling on slot machines. It's intentionally designed to get you addicted. You can hear the people in Las Vegas now. "Just one more pull and I'll win big. Big money big money!" Only that's not the case. On almost every pull, your chance of winning is infinitesimally small.

The infinite scroll creates the same effect. You can hear yourself sitting in sweatpants now. "Just one more scroll and I'll see the best photo, video or status update EVER. New GIF! New GIF!" Only that's not the case. On almost every scroll, it's just another friend somewhere you aren't, someone's abs you don't have, or someone's meal you aren't eating. Just like slot machines, you feel bad you didn't "win." And that's the point. Because you feel bad, you hedge your bets and scroll a little more, certain that this scroll is going to deliver something AMAZING despite knowing deep down that it won't.[113]

It's driven by dopamine, the chemical in our brain that deals with reward, motivation and, – most crucially, alleviating pain. Right when we're on that high of thinking we might get a reward, it spikes. Then when we don't, it plummets. To alleviate that pain, we go for it again, hoping it'll be good this time. Every "like" is a hit and then when the likes stop, we experience a come-down. It can be so attractive, it takes control of us.[114]

For example, your BFF posts a photo from some fabulous beach. REWARD. But oh no, that felt so good. Now you're motivated to find another hit, so you scroll. Oh! Your sister posted a pic of her dinner. Yum! You "like" it. But wait, sad again. Time to alleviate that pain. Scroll a little more. Something else. Like. Come-down. Scroll. Repeat. It's an actual addiction and it's meant to be addictive.

While you're straddled with that emotional rollercoaster, you're being faced with a volume of information like never before and I hate to break it to you, but it's totally messing with your head. Why? Because it's simply more information than our brains can physiologically cope with. Yes, you read that right. We are physically incapable of processing the amount of information we're exposing ourselves to on social media.[115]

We evolved from hunters and gatherers. We were under constant threat from animals and other humans from different groups. We learned to think fast and to do that, we had to assess information quickly, which meant cataloging different things – seeing leaves rustle or hearing footsteps – to literally survive. This programming is still ingrained in us and it is highly effective when there are only a few things – like rustling leaves and the sound of footsteps – stimulating us over and over again.

But what happens when it's a TON of things stimulating us over and over again? Our brain has to make these instantaneous decisions based on things that happened in the past – memories – so we can sort information and move on to the next thing. It's like a giant row of filing cabinets and we've got to get the files in the right draw as quickly as possible.

As this process gets more and more exhausting while we're on our emotional dopamine rollercoaster, we are incentivized to disregard more and more information because it's just too hard. So we prioritise information that reinforces something we already know or believe. For example, "Brexit means taking back control." If we're presented with information that contradicts this – no matter how true it might be – our brain is like "no thank you, that's too hard." But if we get information that reinforces it, our brain is like "thank you so much, that goes in filing cabinet six, second drawer. NEXT!" This is called motivated reasoning and it's a huge part of why we increasingly can't cope with alternative points of view.

When we combine this need to process information quickly to avoid overload with the business model of social media companies to keep us happy with stuff we already like so we stay on longer and they can sell more ads (so they can make more money) , the whole ecosystem starts to make perfect sense. It also becomes increasingly apparent why it's really bad for democracy. In fact, I've come up with a little equation:

Our brain's interest in reinforcing what it already knows + our addiction to the dopamine rollercoaster + social media's incentive to sell as many ads as possible by keeping us happy so we stay online longer = people moving further and further into their own echo chambers just to mentally cope + a total breakdown of shared reality.

Upbeat, right?

NO, YOU DON'T HAVE COMPLETE CONTROL OVER YOUR ACTIONS

—

Now I've explained how all of this messes with your brain, I've got to break a really hard truth to you. You don't have full control over your decision-making. I know it's hard to believe and I'm sure you don't want to accept it but that's reality. Human beings are influenced by stuff. Think about your favourite pair of shoes. Do you think you bought them entirely of your own volition? Unlikely. No doubt you saw an ad, or 5,000. A friend might have had them. Someone you thought was attractive might have been wearing them in the street. Whatever the reason, your decision took into account dozens if not hundreds of stimuli.

You might concede this point but still think to yourself "that's not true when it comes to politics!" That view is built on your ego and these companies – who want to make as much money as possible – telling you over and over again, "of course you're in total control because you're amazing!" It feels good to think we're the masters of our own destiny. Unfortunately, you'd be wrong. Politics is marketing just like anything else. It's feeling part of a group in the form of a political party. It's having an "us" that is against a "them". It's childhood memories of your parent's point of view. It's how you feel about the candidate. And it's ads, newspaper articles, comments, shares and likes on social media repeated over and over in an ever-shrinking echo chamber that is built to capitalize on how your brain works to keep you on the platform as long as possible to sell as many ads as possible. After all, you're the product.

WHY IT'S BAD

DEMOCRACY DEPENDS ON DISCOURSE

—

Before we get to how we fix this mess, we need to geek out briefly on some political theory. There was this brilliant German philosopher named Jurgen Habermas who came up with the theory of the public sphere, which he defined as "an area in social life where individuals can come together to freely discuss and identify societal problems, and through that discussion influence political action". In short, it's how a group of people – most likely citizens of the same country – get together to discuss how they want things to be. In older times it was Britain's coffee houses and the salons of Paris. In more modern times, it was through media like radio and television. Today, it's increasingly on social media.

The most important part of this theory is the role that power plays. Who gets to participate and how? Systemic racism in the U.S. and in countries around the world continues to exclude a large portion of society. Sexism, homophobia, transphobia, Islamaphobia, Anti-Semitism, ableism, classism, and other forms of discrimination do the same for other marginalised groups. If you're a rich straight white cisgender man though, you're probably doing just fine even though it might feel like – from social media – you aren't. It's all part of the plan.

While addressing those issues is for another book (and many exist already, so go read them), one key aspect remains true: Our ability to deal with societal problems requires us to be in a shared reality. We've all got to be working from the same facts. While there will always be some disparity, we have largely – until the last decade – been exposed to similar sources of information. In fact, information collection itself was a group activity. In 1988, the UK public service broadcasters (BBC, ITV and Channel 4) accounted for 100% of TV news viewing.[116] When people went out into the public sphere, they were dealing with a fairly shared reality.

As the internet emerged and access to information was "democratized", it initially felt like a good thing. More people could get more information and therefore more people could engage in the public sphere. Seemingly good. But like anything, powerful actors started to monopolize control of that information. Google with search. Twitter with "on the pulse" information. Facebook and its companies with a vast majority of all social media interactions. Suddenly the thing that was supposed to give more power to more people became more consolidated than any medium in modern history; and that medium's interest isn't in informing the public so it can function as one society. It's in selling as many ads as possible.

In 2022, 46% of people in the UK used social media for news despite those same people saying it was the least trustworthy of all news sources.[117] This reliance is fueled by its addictive nature and its algorithmic drive to feed people stuff that confirms what they want to believe instead of broadly informing them of objective truth. This has driven people deeper and deeper into isolated, reaffirming echo chambers and driven society further away from any semblance of a shared reality, making democratic discourse all but impossible.

Interestingly, viewing figures in the UK for BBC, ITV and Channel 4 news surged during the COVID-19 pandemic after years of decline.[118] In a crisis, people clearly crave proper, trustworthy news. And they know they're not going to get it from social media.

Yet whether we like it or not, the new public sphere is online – and not just online but mostly on Facebook. Yet there is almost no regulation or independent oversight. In the short span of fifteen years we've ceded power of the primary space people "come together to freely discuss and identify societal problems" to a business model that prioritises profit above all else, with no democratic accountability. Does that seem right to you?

SOCIAL MEDIA IS BAD FOR YOUR HEALTH

—

It's time to define some really important terms. First, misinformation, which is false or inaccurate information. Basically, a lie about something real. This differs from disinformation, which is misinformation that has been intentionally manufactured and spread with the intention of obscuring the truth and influencing public opinion.[119] Basically, something that's intentionally made up. Attempting to constantly differentiate between the two can be confusing and does more harm than good because we end up arguing over a nuanced point instead of focusing on the bigger, looming threat. As such, I will refer to all of it as disinformation.

The spread of disinformation is done by companies, organisations or individuals in order to achieve financial, political or ideological gain.[120] Basically, bad people doing bad things for their own personal benefit. Sound familiar?

Disinformation has been particularly prevalent during the COVID-19 pandemic, with false stories about the virus spreading widely online. These have covered a variety of areas, from false (and often dangerous) information about "miracle" cures to conspiracy theories about 5G's role in spreading infection or the virus' origins in a secret laboratory. This disinformation has imperiled lives and will – as we move forward into a world where effective treatments and vaccines are developed – make it even harder for society to recover.[121]

Ironically, disinformation behaves exactly like a virus.[122] It requires:

1. A **source**.

2. People susceptible to infection.

3. A way to **transmit** from person to person.

The source of disinformation can be anyone, from your weird uncle to the President of the United States. It is, however, often incubated in the more obscure parts of the internet and then spread from there into the "normal" bits. Some particularly organised disinformation "influencers" (not the good kind) have professionalised the manufacture of disinformation. It is well reported, for example, that organisations working for the Russian state employ "bots" – fake social media accounts – to amplify and spread disruptive stories. These have been very active during the COVID-19 pandemic and it is estimated that bots are responsible for 70% of COVID-19 activity on Twitter.[123] To repeat, fake social media accounts are responsible for over two-thirds of all COVID-19 activity on Twitter.

Who are the people susceptible to disinformation? All of us. The creators of false stories know just how to make them believable and likely to trend. Older people are far more susceptible largely because they're more likely to treat stuff they've seen online with the same repute as something they've read in a major newspaper.[124] Disinformation is often presented like proper news and usually sensationalist in tone, like a tabloid newspaper such as *The National Enquirer* or *The Daily Mail*.

Transmission of the disinformation virus occurs because of the way social media platforms are designed. The platforms are meant to be addictive and the algorithms that drive them are set up to promote content that is engaged with, rather than content that is trustworthy or verified. Social media companies, unlike traditional news media, do very little to edit what is on their platforms. Numerous studies have shown that people are more likely to believe a story if the source is their friends and if they are exposed to it repeatedly.[125] It is a dangerous combination.

The former President of the United States has had COVID-19 content he's posted on Facebook, Twitter and YouTube removed because it is disinformation.[126] The "5G cell phone towers are causing COVID-19" conspiracy has led people to set fire to dozens of these towers across the UK.[127] Another suggested Bill Gates was going to reduce the world's population by sterilizing people with a COVID-19 vaccine.[128] On

Facebook as a whole, misleading health content had over 3.8 billion views over the past year, peaking during the COVID-19 pandemic. The 10 most viewed sites sharing disinformation had nearly four times as many views as content from the 10 leading health institutions in April 2020 alone.[129] On balance then, consuming 'public health information' on social media was more likely to get you ill than it was to help you stay safe.

FEELINGS AREN'T FACTS

—

Your Facebook feed, Instagram feed and Twitter feed are a totally unique thing on this planet. No other person has an identical feed. It's made just for you and the more you use it, the more "customised" it gets. There's no adversity and there's nothing that challenges you because the goal is to keep you there as long as possible. It's the ultimate exercise in self-absorption and the "culture of me." This strokes our ego. It makes us feel special. We believe we're correct all the time and we're less and less inclined to compromise.

Because social media is fueled by keeping people on as long as possible by whatever means necessary, it has fueled a culture of validating people's feelings, whatever they might be. The way social media jumbles up subjective personal things ("Yay, my sister had a baby and I'm happy!") with objective things ("The earth is round, I swear"), has begun to mix up how we feel about something with the facts about something.

For example, I was having a conversation with someone about the UK's National Health Service. The suggestion was made that the United States couldn't do something similar because it's "just too big." I suggested that perhaps it could work at state level. The person I was speaking to was from Pennsylvania and they said "well the population of Pennsylvania is about the same as the UK." I politely noted that it was, in fact, not even close. The population of Pennsylvania is 12.8 million people. The population of the UK is 66.8 million people. I even showed him census data. His response? "Well I grew up there and it feels like the population is about the same."

How you feel about a fact doesn't make that fact any more or less true. I feel that eating ice cream for every meal of the day should be healthy but that doesn't make it true. Eating ice cream for every meal of the day will make me overweight and likely give me diabetes.

NIKES, REEBOKS, THE FUTURE OF HUMANITY. IT'S ALL THE SAME, RIGHT?

———

Let's be clear: There are HUGE issues with the global advertising industry and the harmful hypercapitalism that underpins it but again, that's a different book. For the sake of this book – and for the sake of humanity – I'm hoping we can all agree that selling shoes is very different than affecting the outcome of a democratic election with disinformation. That's exactly what a range of nefarious actors have been trying to do with social media.

The reasons are logical from their perspective-- It's great value for money. Facebook ads, and even better, using a massive number of fake accounts (Facebook took down over 5.4 BILLION fake accounts in 2019)[130] combined with bots on Twitter (Twitter takes down over 100 million bots each year)[131] and a network of seemingly legitimate news sources to create the appearance of organic support is cheap! Combine that with easily abused liberal values like free speech and you've got the perfect environment to sow chaos and convince millions of people they're living in an alternate reality that doesn't exist.

We know this already happened. Almost every US intelligence agency agreed that Russia attempted to influence the 2016 US Presidential election in support of Donald Trump.[132] Thankfully, when he became President, Donald Trump set up a task force to combat Russian influence and ensure that we safeguarded future elections to preserve our delicate institutions and way of life. Just kidding! He did nothing. So much nothing that the Russians did it again in 2020.[133] The UK, meanwhile, despite mounting evidence of Russian interference in the 2016 Brexit referendum, didn't even bother to really look into it.[134]

It's not all down to Russia though. By the 2020 elections, disinformation lessons had been learned and the US political landscape was full of domestic actors that were just as bad, like the Trump campaign itself.[135] The platforms – powered by algorithms designed to drive people further and further into self-perpetuating echo chambers – enabled and encouraged this behaviour. Instagram even admitted there was a "technical error" in their hashtag system that boosted negative hashtags about Biden while hiding them for Trump. Was there any punishment for doing this? Of course not![136]

All the power, no responsibility.

2023? MORE LIKE 1984

—

I was born in 1984, the year in which George Orwell's dystopian novel of the same name is set. If you haven't read it, I'll sum it up for you in three words: Oh My God! The citizens of Oceania are ruled by the "Party," which is led by "Big Brother". Devotion to the party supersedes everything. Truth isn't truth. Truth is whatever the party says is true. If the party says black is white, then black is white. There's a loudspeaker and microphone in everyone's home, always recording. Cameras in every room, always recording. People's movements are monitored. Where they go. When they go. Who they're with.

Orwell said he modeled this dystopia on Stalin's Soviet Union; and the book is often used as a reference point for other authoritarian countries like China. From their "tech eyes" program set up to monitor behaviour and dissent[137] to a new social credit system where everyone starts with 1,000 points and can gain more by doing good things like volunteering but lose points for doing bad things like running a red light[138], China can often seem like the archetype for chilling tech-authoritarianism.

We frame these programs as "shocking" and "illiberal" in North America and Europe, yet the vast majority of people in both place have a smartphone – a device we carry with us at all times that tracks our every move, listens to us when we talk, and holds all of our photos, emails and messages – often in a remote "cloud" owned and controlled by a big corporation. We've put "smart" speakers in our homes that listen to our conversations and most intimate moments. Video cameras in our living rooms to call our family and friends. "Smart" fridges in our kitchens that track and store when we open the fridge door and when we're low on milk. Cars that are effectively computers with wheels that can go into "autopilot" mode and drive us around nearly unassisted. Watches that measure our heart rates and our oxygen levels and keep track of how many steps we take.

Every one of these activities creates data about us. Who we're with. Who we speak to. Where we are. When we're there. *Who we are*. And the company that sold us that gadget – or the company that provides a service in exchange for being allowed to turn us into a product they then sell – owns all of that data. They own you.

At the same time, we read about how old people in nursing homes are being "kept company" by robots and think it's lovely.[139] Why don't we just go visit them? Horror stories of an algorithm determining kids' exam grades based on their postcodes, further ingraining racism and classism.[140] Or how the UK Government's tech-driven, algorithmic overhaul of its welfare system is actively impoverishing the very people it was designed to help.[141] Elon Musk tells us we have to get computer chips implanted in our brains so robots don't take us over, seeming to forget that we invented the robots in the first place and can stop whenever we want.[142] Technological advances aren't progress if they risk our own human future.

This wasn't forced upon us. We didn't agree to this after being dragged kicking and screaming. No, we opted in. By our own volition. By choice. We've been convinced that we made these decisions ourselves. That we have free will and we used it to consent to this way of life. It started innocently enough. Accepting terms and conditions that were simple to begin with. Slowly but surely, new features were added. We're asked to give access to our microphone. Then our camera and our contacts. With each new feature came more terms and more conditions, though we were rarely – if ever – asked to opt-in every time something changed.

And that's the con. What choice do we *really* have?" The power lies not in deciding between two imperfect options – an iPhone or an Android – but in determining what options you can choose from to begin with. In our modern world the question is not "do you want a smartphone or not," it's "which smartphone will you get?" Opting out of technology is akin to opting out of society. It's not an option. So we have to demand that the technology is made better.

WHAT YOU CAN DO ABOUT IT

ASSESSING YOUR DIGITAL LIFE

You, like me, may find that last bit terrifying. But as we've learned, fear is good. It motivates us. There are no quick fixes and my ultimate recommendations may seem extreme, but so are the challenges facing us. So let's get to work.

To give you an idea of what apps collect the most data on you, here's a non-exhaustive list (because there's just too many to name). Don't worry, I'm going to suggest some alternatives a bit further down! Here goes:

❖ Google: Android operating system, Google Search, Chrome browser, Gmail, Google Maps, Youtube, Chromebook computers, Google Classroom, Google Assistant and Nest. Basically, every Google product.

❖ Microsoft: Minecraft, Xbox Live, LinkedIn, Word, Excel, Outlook and the whole 365 Suite of software.

❖ Amazon: The store which keeps track of everything you've ever bought and watched (on Prime video), Alexa speakers and Ring Doorbells and cameras.

❖ Apple: Safari web browser and iPhone (location data)

❖ Miscellaneous Apps: Slack, most web browsers, banking apps and healthcare apps . For example, apps that track the size of an unborn baby. Yes, some of those are selling data about your unborn child to a third party. **That means your kid has a digital "footprint" before they can make an actual one.**

When it comes to smartphones, all are not created equal with regard to privacy. The real issue isn't so much the device but the operating system. The two most common operating systems are iOS (on Apple devices like iPhones and iPad) and Android (part of Google and likely on your device if it isn't made by Apple). With Android, every aspect of the device is designed to collect data on you. That's the point, unfortunately. While iOS isn't perfect, it's much better and the newest updates give you a lot more power to protect your privacy.

Below, I've outlined the most common instructions for both iPhones and Android devices and the most common apps but, understandably, these may not apply to your devices. Again, please don't hate-Tweet @ me because I didn't cover the type of phone you have. Just do an internet search for your device and whatever you want to do. That's the good thing about the internet-- it covers everything.

You can start fixing your digital life by securing your own personal tracking device (aka your smartphone):

❖ Make sure you have a passcode that keeps it locked and secure.

 ◈ If you have an iPhone:

  ✦ Go to "Settings", then go to "Face ID & Passcode" (or "Touch ID and Passcode" for iPhone 8 and earlier models), then select "Change Passcode"

  ✦ On the screen where you're asked to enter a new passcode, tap on "Passcode Options" which should appear right above the number pad after you've entered your old passcode

  ✦ Select "Custom Alphanumeric Code". This will allow you to use numbers, letters, and special characters in your passcode, which you can use to create a cryptic, random code that only you know and no one has a chance of guessing. You should also consider disabling Face ID if its enabled

 ◈ If you have an Android:

  ✦ Avoid using pattern or pin passcodes, and go for the password option, which is the strongest of the three (make sure it's random and uses numbers, letters and special characters). This can be done by opening

your Google account, selecting "Security",
and then "Signing into your Account"

✦ Turn on 2-step verification. Do this by
opening your Google account, selecting
"Security" in the navigation panel, tapping
"Signing into Google", locating "2 Step
Verification", and following the on-screen
steps

✦ Disable Auto-Sign In. This can be done
by again opening your Google account,
selecting "Security", "Signing into Other
Sites", and toggling the slider labeled "Auto
Sign-in"

❖ Disable Cookies in your browser:

◇ On Google Chrome, click the three vertical
dots in the top right corner of the page, and
select "Settings". On the left hand side, locate
and click on "Privacy and Security". Scroll
down to "Cookies and other site data". Enable
the options to "Block third-party cookies",
"Clear cookies and site data when you close
all windows", and "Send a do-not-track
request with your browsing traffic".
Alternatively, you can just select "Block All
Cookies", though this will affect functionality
of some websites. However, this is definitely
the safer option.

- ✧ On Firefox, click the menu button and select "Preferences". Go to the "privacy and Security" panel, and either select the "Strict" option or the "Custom" option. In "Custom", you can choose to block either all third-party cookies or all cookies generally. FIrefox is a great browser option, generally speaking.

- ✧ On Safari, go to the Safari tab on the top left of your screen and select "Preferences". Click privacy, and then select "Prevent Cross-site tracking". Alternatively, you can just select "Block all cookies", again this will affect functionality of certain sites, but your privacy is worth it

- ❖ On iPhone, ask all apps "not to track" when prompted by the phone. That's right, apps on your phone (like Facebook) track your activity across the entire device, building massive profiles about you in the background that are then stored and used to target ads to you. Tell them no!

- ❖ Disable Cookies on your phone:

  - ✧ On iPhone: Launch Safari. Select "Preferences", click on "Privacy" and then "Block All Cookies". Confirm the warning message.

  - ✧ On Android: Launch Chrome. Tap the

menu icon, then go to "Settings". Tap "Site Settings", then "Cookies" and then toggle "Cookies" to turn them off.

❖ Get an encrypted password tool to safely store all your passwords & upgrade your passwords.

    ◈ 1Password and LastPass are great options

    ◈ Change all your passwords so they're cryptic. None of this "MyName@567!" nonsense

❖ Turn off location services for every app that really doesn't need it. Only Maps really needs it.

    ◈ On iPhone, go to "Settings", then "Privacy", then "Location Services". You should see a list of apps on your phone – find Maps and Google Maps and select "While Using the App". For everything else, you can select "Never" or "Ask Next Time"

    ◈ On Android, open up your "Settings" tab, select "Location", and then go to "App Permissions". For Google Maps, you can select "Only While Using the App", and select "Never" or "Ask Next Time" for everything else

❖ Even on maps, turn off saving your every move (that's the default setting) and delete the stored history of your location.

    ◈ For Apple Maps on iPhone, go to your

THE LITTLE BLACK BOOK OF SOCIAL MEDIA

iPhone Settings, go to "Privacy", then "Location Services", then scroll all the way down to "System Services". Scroll down to "Significant Locations" and toggle it to turn it off.

✧ For Google Maps on iPhone and Android, open the app and select your profile picture (or just the circle with the first letter of your name in it), then go to "Your Data in Maps". Toggle the slider entitled "Location History" to turn it off. It will remain off until you choose to turn it back on

❖ Turn off "Hey Siri" and "Okay Google" voice assistants

✧ If you have an iPhone, go to "Settings", then "Siri and Search". Turn off the sliders that say "Listen for Hey Siri", and "Press Side Button for Siri".

✧ If you have an Android, touch and hold the "Home" button, tap "more" (three dots on the top right), and select "Turn off Google Assistant".

❖ Turn off microphone and camera access for every app that doesn't absolutely need it.

✧ On iPhone, go to "Settings", then "Privacy", and then "Camera". Use the sliders to turn it off for every app that doesn't need it (which is most of them). Do the same for "Microphone", which is also located in "Privacy"

✧ On Android, go to your settings and select "Privacy". Then go to "Permission Manager". In there you will find a "Camera" and "Microphone" option. Go into each one and toggle the sliders for the apps that do not need it (again, most of them)

✧ Delete social media apps and use mobile web instead. You don't need the app! The sites are way more clunky on mobile, which will help you spend less time on them.

Next, let's look at other aspects of your digital life:

❖ Ask yourself, "do I really need a "smart" speaker to turn on my lights and set a timer? Spoiler alert: The answer is NO. It might be convenient but is it worth giving a company tons of data on your routines and possibly letting them listen in to your every word? Get rid of them.

❖ Take a long hard look at every other aspect of your life that you've digitized. I'm not going to tell you what to keep and what to get rid of. Ask yourself "is there an analog version (like a good old-fashioned watch) that can do the job I need as opposed to the job I've been told I want?" as

THE LITTLE BLACK BOOK OF SOCIAL MEDIA

well as "Is this bit of tech worth the data about me it'll give to a company or government?"

Finally, let's consider social media:

❖ Facebook

   ✧ Really, what is it bringing to your life? Write down the aspects of Facebook that you can replace with something else. Would a secure messaging tool and a secure photo-sharing tool do instead? Download a reputable news app to get your information instead of picking it up from people's shares in your news feed. Perhaps you decide you can't live without Facebook. That's fine too, but at least you'll have considered it. At the very least then, lock down your privacy settings. Here's how:

     ✦ Go to Facebook.com and login. Find "Settings" in the drop down menu on the right hand side of the page. Locate "Privacy", and click on it. For every option on the list, you can click "Edit" and change the settings so that only you, or only select people can see the relevant information. "Only Me" is always the most secure option. Additionally, go to the "Timeline and Tagging" settings, to control who can tag you in posts and post on your timeline.

❖ If you do decide to delete it, here's how:

  ✦ Find "Settings" in the drop down menu on the right hand side of the webpage. Go to "General", then "Manage Your Account", select "Deactivate Your Account", then confirm the decision.

❖ Other social media sites

  ✧ From Twitter to Instagram and everything else, make the same assessments as above and act on them.

  ✧ Is this making you feel a bit anxious? They start with a 30-day challenge. Pick one platform – let's say Facebook first – and stop using it. It'll be hard at first, but if you stick with it and you aren't craving it at the end of the challenge, then don't look back and free yourself of it! Once you've gotten rid of one, try a second. Then a third. This is a process!

❖ Web Browsing and Search

  ✧ If you log into Chrome with your Google account, you can kiss privacy goodbye. Instead install the DuckDuckGo extension. They don't collect or share ANY personal information. They've got their own browser for mobile as well. On mobile, use the DuckDuckGo browser app. It is privacy first.

❖ Email

    ✦ Consider ProtonMail. It's end-to-end encrypted.

❖ Secure messaging

    ✦ If you're using iMessage, that's encrypted, so well done you!

    ✦ WhatsApp is owned by Facebook. Avoid it!

    ✦ Signal is an independent, encrypted, messaging service. Give it a try!

❖ Privacy

    ✦ Jumbo: Security + Privacy is an app that allows you to see what data other applications on your device are taking. It can help you block trackers in apps, delete social media posts and more. It's not free, which is a good indication you're not the product!

Hopefully the above will help you start to secure your digital life. In reality, this stuff is hard. We've become used to these tools. They're part of our everyday lives and they're almost like an extension of ourselves. There's also digital inclusion to think about. It is difficult, now, to be a part of modern society if we don't engage with digital tools and platforms, but we can be more discerning about the sites and tools we use. That's the first – and most important – step.

But the responsibility shouldn't be entirely on us. These platforms were designed to be the way they are. If humans designed it this way, then humans can redesign it. It's high time we pushed our governments to start making the tech giants design with humanity in mind.

FIXING DATA

The phrase "fixing data" carries a great deal more weight than those two words might suggest. We're talking about a commodity that is now more valuable than oil[143] and an industry that is in its infancy. There are concrete steps we can take now, however, to curb the harmful effects of data while we work to get a grasp on the bigger problems.

They relate particularly to the algorithms driven by artificial intelligence that use data to deliver content to people. We know they're designed to inch people further and further to the extremes so we could redesign them so they don't do that. We could also overlay algorithms with a certain percentage of 'universal' content so no matter what level of extreme your personal content moves towards, at least a certain percentage would be the same across the board. That would help get us back to some semblance of shared reality. We could also force companies to publish their algorithms so we know what's happening behind the scenes.

The fundamental problem with the role of data in modern society, however, is rooted in the imbalance of power between individuals and the large companies that control our 'data-selves'. It's a dynamic that doesn't really exist in any other aspect of our economy and it stems from the "tech exception" – the ideas that technology companies are somehow benevolent, good and different than any other businesses. We must accept this is not true. These companies are some of the largest, most profitable businesses in the history of the world.

What makes them different is that they wouldn't have a product without us because *we are their product.* They sell our attention to advertisers and reap the rewards, believing the service they provide us with is compensation enough.

We need to enshrine in law that a person's digital identity – their data – is their property. This would rebalance the power dynamic and allow individuals to seek fair compensation for the value they add to these companies. Without us, they're worthless. Tim Berners-Lee, the inventor of the world-wide web (that "www" before every website) calls these "pods," people's very own online data stores.[144]

Because this value is derived from the value of our collective data, individuals could join data unions with representative leaders to negotiate the value of a user's data, building an equitable foundation for a sustainable business model.

My Data, My Rights.

SAVING DEMOCRACY

—

If you've read the entire book you'll likely have come to the same conclusion as me. Privately owned, profit-driven and data-dependent, the business models of companies like Facebook, Twitter and Google are not compatible with the fundamental needs of a liberal democracy: an informed citizenry living in a shared reality. Too often we accept reality as it is, trying to tweak the edges and forgetting that we created the problem in the first place rather than attempting to conceive of a new reality that we have the power to create.

There are practical things we can all do in the short-term while we fight for fundamental change. For example you can **become a Bot Warrior**:

❖ **Step 1: Identify the bots**

⬧ They post a lot – the Oxford internet Institute's Computational Propaganda team views an average of more than 50 posts a day as suspicious;

⬧ Their profile is "sparse" – there is no header photo, the profile pic looks generic, etc. – the less personal information on the profile, the more likely it is to be a bot;

- ✦ Their ratio of followers to following is really off balance. If they're following 500+ people but only have 3 followers, be suspicious;

- ✦ There are really basic typos, spelling and grammar errors.

❖ Step 2: Report the bots

- ✦ Report the bots using the social media company's reporting function. Facebook takes down billions of "fake" accounts every year.[145]

- ✦ Do not: 1) retweet 2) reply to 3) follow them. It only "ups" their value to the platform's algorithm.

While bots cannot compare in scale to the all-pervasive nature of Google, Facebook, Amazon and others, it is at least *something* we can all do.

A report my organisation Fair Vote UK published in early 2020[146] outlined the ways Governments could start to tackle this problem:

- ❖ Regulate (or totally ban) the ability of campaigns to target voters based on personal data.

- ❖ Require digital imprints on online political adverts.

- ❖ Include market-based costs of datasets in spending regulations.

❖ Create a digital ad depository of all online political advertisements.

❖ Create, support and resource our regulatory organisations.

❖ Support and resource fact-checking organisations.

❖ Provide long-term digital education campaigns (for all members of society, not just the young).

I could outline a further litany of proposals to safeguard elections and defend our democratic systems.[147] While all these changes would help, the companies – with their billions of dollars and deep political influence – would find ways to delay reform and circumvent regulations because many of them are – at present – more powerful than most, if not all, governments on the planet. There is some hope at the moment. The attempted coup at the US Capitol on January 6th forced many legislators to wake up to the power of big tech as their own lives were at risk. Several places have rejected proposals from Google and others to turn their municipalities into full-scale surveillance "smart cities."[148] Still, despite the mounting evidence of the dangers posed by big tech, there are serious efforts to give them *more* power, like in Nevada, USA. According to drafts of Governor Sisolak's proposed legislation, a new classification would be introduced called "Innovation Zones," where tech companies would be allowed to form their own local governments that would have the same level of authority as a traditional county entity. They could impose taxes, create judicial systems, school districts and even deliver 'government' services.[149]

Mark Zuckerberg, owner of Facebook, is arguably the most powerful person in the world right now. He essentially controls a majority share of the company that decides what nearly 3 billion people on the planet see everyday. If Facebook were a country, it would be nearly twice as populous as China and equally authoritarian, with absolute decision-making in the hands of Mark Zuckerberg.

In an effort to draw attention away from this reality, Facebook set up its own Supreme Court. It's remit, however, doesn't cover any of the root causes. All it can really consider are content decisions. For example, this body was given the power to decide whether Donald Trump should be permanently banned.[150] Regardless of whether you think his ban should remain or not (with a decision likely before publication of this book), decisions of this scale should not be in the hands of a private, extrajudicial body with no democratic oversight. We have to ask ourselves, should any one company – or any one person for that matter – particularly one who is not democratically elected – really have this much power?

As a result of the recent series of major conflicts facilitated by social media companies, some governments are pursuing comprehensive regulation. In Europe, the Digital Services and Markets Act aims to tackle both the near monopolistic power of big tech companies alongside new requirements on the management of both illegal and harmful but legal speech[151]. The United Kingdom is taking a similar approach with its Online Safety Bill, though it has been dogged by delays related to appeasing the right-wing absolute free speech lobby. This group simultaneously acknowledges these companies are private enterprises but seek to demand universal and unfettered access.[152] In the United States, the primary avenue of change has been to pursue the break-up of large tech companies. For example, forcing Meta to sell Instagram and WhatsApp while retaining Facebook.[153]

To save democracy we have to reimagine what an informed society looks like and create it ourselves urgently. That world doesn't include an entity like Facebook or YouTube or Twitter in its current form. To fix the problem, we must eliminate the financial incentive that allows hate for profit and we must get out of this myopic conversation of absolute free speech, which has never been the case. Even when someone is entitled to freedom of speech, they are not inherently entitled to freedom of *reach* enabled by social media.

We need to start thinking much bigger. Why can't a social network be publicly owned or treated as a public utility, with the prime objective of facilitating information and engagement? That's what governments do. From firefighters to teachers, we accept that some things are more important than corporate profit. A digital public sphere that helps society function should also be one of them. It's time for our governments to act and it is up to all of us to make them.

SECURING OUR FUTURE

If you look at the world today, it feels unrecognizable to what it looked like only five years ago. Few of us could have imagined the rate at which things could unravel. We had faith in our institutions and in the rule of law but we failed to understand just how delicate they are.

The great irony of our way of life is that the endgame is the antithesis of the system itself. The end result of democracy is authoritarianism. If you "win" at it enough, then you're a dictator. Let's say, for example, in the United States one party wins the Presidency, holds over 60 seats in the Senate, controls the House of Representatives and controls the legislature of 38 states. This could all be achieved without winning a majority of votes because of the nature of the system. This tyranny of the minority could lead to calling a convention, rewriting the constitution and ending American democracy as we know it *using American democracy to do it.*

The same is true for capitalism. The end-game of free-market competition is monopoly. If there are 10 airlines and one is much better, the other nine close and you don't have choice anymore. That company now controls all of air travel. That's exactly what's happened to most of the internet. We can't take the old and new 'sacred' institutions of democracy for granted and we must remember that they have to be nurtured. Tended to. Managed. There is no invisible hand.

Right now, we find ourselves in the midst of a global pandemic that has already claimed the lives of more than two million people around the world and has driven tens of millions into grinding poverty. Meanwhile, America's billionaires added $1.3 trillion to their personal wealth since the pandemic began. We're reaching an inequality inflection point that was last seen at the turn of the 20th Century. As more and more people find themselves with less and less, populists and fascists provide simple solutions to complex problems, like suggesting immigration is the root cause of rising unemployment. Because this isn't actually the cause, further chaos ensues. A chaos that manages to confirm the message in an endless feedback loop.

One of the core tenets of public history is that knowledge of the past is essential to avoid the repetition of mistakes. So how did we get here? The answer is simple: our elected representatives and indeed a significant majority of the general public remain ignorant to the power of tech giants.

Their products are addictive, their motive is solely to make money and their infrastructure – how they work – is incredibly technical and complicated. Even when we have clear examples of their harm, like their role in a genocide in south-east Asia or, closer to home, boosting COVID disinformation, we struggle to believe that we are being manipulated.

At the same time, we have become worryingly disconnected from the fact that human beings are animals on this planet just like any other creature. Our primary goal as a species is to ensure that we continue as a species. Yet we have spent most of our history splitting into groups based on socially constructed concepts. From tribes to nation-states, we've pitted ourselves in endless conflicts. Now, we face an immediate threat in the form of COVID-19 alongside the greatest threat to ever challenge our species: climate change. It will only be tackled if we work together and yet the world is more divided than ever.

There has been only one major shift in how we engage with one another as human beings since everything really started falling apart and it is the rise of social media. Our very survival depends on us finding a way back to a shared reality. A society where we are living in the *same* world, because it's the only one we have. Let's get to work.

ACKNOWLEDGEMENTS

—

This book was first written in the depth of COVID-19 lockdown. As the world seemed to stop turning, social media became a primary outlet for people to connect. As its role increased, so did its impact on elections, society and democracy.

First acknowledgments to you, the reader! Thanks for buying my book, especially after I was told I "didn't have enough Twitter followers" to get a book published. My, how our world has changed. Let's not let Twitter followers become the only metric for expertise and knowledge.

First and foremost thanks to Nico, my first edition researcher, cheerleader and indispensable right hand who made this whole thing possible. To Matt Gallagher as well, who intricately outlined the vivid details of how to protect your digital life and kept the entire second edition of this book up-to-date as the issues I covered were changing daily.

Thanks to Astrid, my Belgian sister of seventeen years, who managed to translate my cover and layout ideas into the first edition of this book and formed the look and feel for the entire Little Black Book series, and to Steve Laird, who has evolved the design brilliantly.

Chris, Shahmir, Mark and Carole – you inspired a movement for change and justice that isn't going away. To the OG Fair Vote UK crew – Atalandi, Baroness Benjamin, Elle, Ian and Sara – what a wild ride. You're legends. Everybody's got a little outlaw in 'em.

Susan Schoenfeld-Harrington, you put me under your wing and have enabled and supported me so much. Thank you for everything, especially the fabulous title idea! I am eternally grateful. David G, you're wise, you're supportive and you're generous. Thank you. Aditi, Lisa and Sarah, thanks for that early draft read! Maria, thanks for that second draft read and all those tips! Roger, thanks for reading several drafts to make sure I included every important, frightening thing possible.

Damian, Stephen, Caroline and Deidre, keep up the fight! Stephen C, Peter, Joachim, Caolan, George, Hardeep and Ella – you made this possible. Thank you.

Thanks to my Dad, aka Walt, who was the inspiration for this book and an inspiration in life. He's the hardest working person I know. And to my Mom who is the single most supportive, thoughtful and kind human. Chelsey and Cody, it's a privilege to be your big brother. Five by five. Brandon and Chase, you somehow opted into this madhouse of a family. Thanks for listening to my holiday rants about capitalism, white supremacy and the patriarchy.

Thanks to SAK, the Fab Five, Tokyo Gremlin, Europhiles, the Cottage crew, Freedom isn't Free, Little Kyle and Liggy, my chosen family who accept me exactly as I am – loud, opinionated and often a bit EXTRA.

Anne, Robin, Tamsin, Susan, Gail, Tiffany, Ann and Ann – you've been my surrogate mothers, supporters and wisdom-holders. You're my village and you help me keep it together.

Nan and Steve, there are no words.

Paul, thanks for putting up with me through the strangest year anyone could possibly have imagined.

To my Papa, who took a risk and immigrated half-way around the world so generations after him could have a better life. At 92, you are an inspiration.

And finally to Dorey and my Nana, who both taught me to live life like nobody is watching. I miss you both every day.

ENDNOTES

1 For the full story check out Chris Wylie's excellent tell-all account of the whole sorry episode: *Mindf*ck: Cambridge Analytica and the Plot to Break America* (London: Random House, 2019).

2 Cadwalladr, Carole, 'The Vote Leave scandal, one year on: 'the whole thing was traumatic'', *The Guardian*, 17th March 2019. https://bit.ly/33dPA7G

3 Facebook, 'Preparing for Election Day', *Facebook Newsroom,* 7th October 2020. https://bit.ly/38clm7N

4 Graham, Megan & Rodriguez, Salvador, 'Twitter and Facebook Race to label a slew of posts making false election claims before all votes counted', *CNBC News,* 4th November 2020. https://cnb.cx/358iQxv

5 Silverman, Craig & Mac, Ryan, 'Facebook Knows That Adding Labels To Trump's False Claims Does Little To Stop Their Spread', *Buzzfeed News,* 16th November 2020. https://bit.ly/3hETbRO

6 Clegg, Nick (@nick_clegg), 18th December, 2020. https://bit.ly/3pPKzuO

7 Beckett, Lois & Wong, Julia, 'The misinformation media machine amplifying Trump's election lies', *The Guardian,* 10th November 2020. https://bit.ly/3j0hdax

8 Yourish, Karen, Buchanan, Larry & Lu, Denise, 'The 147 Republicans Who Voted to Overturn Election Results' *The New York Times,* 7th January 2021. https://nyti.ms/3r5uRwe

9 Lonsdorf, Kat, et al. 'A Timeline of How the Jan. 6 Attack Unfolded — Including Who Said What and When'. *NPR*, 9th June 2022. https://n.pr/3YzCGeV

10 *Ibid.*

11 Dwoskin, Elizabeth, 'Facebook's Sandberg Deflected Blame for Capitol Riot, but New Evidence Shows How Platform Played Role', *The Washington Post*, 29th October 2022. https://wapo.st/3W8tJHU

12 *Ibid*

13 Crowley, James, '"Stop the Steal" Facebook Group Taken Down After Attracting 300,000 Members in Two Days', *Newsweek*, 5th November 2020. https://bit.ly/3YBBfwF

14 Brewster, Thomas, 'Sheryl Sandberg Downplayed Facebook's Role In The Capitol Hill Siege—Justice Department Files Tell A Very Different Story', *Forbes*, 7th February 2021. https://bit.ly/3jjWvHb

15 *Ibid.*

16 Frenkel, Sheera, 'The pro-Bolsonaro riot and Jan. 6 attack followed a similar digital playbook, experts say', *The New York Times*, 9th January 2023. shorturl.at/wKLZ7

17 Mahoney, Adam, 'Armed white men patrolling Kenosha protests organized on Facebook', *The Guardian,* 26th August 2020. https://bit.ly/3obKtwU

18 Rodriguez, Salvador, 'Zuckerberg says Facebook's failure to remove Kenosha militia page was 'an operational mistake'', *CNBC News,* 28th August 2020. https://cnb.cx/3rZTpbh

19 Global Witness, 'Facebook Approves Adverts Containing Hate Speech Inciting Violence and Genocide against the Rohingya'. *Global Witness*, 20th March 2022. https://bit.ly/3PFZp4Y

20 Miles, Tom, 'U.N. Investigators Cite Facebook Role in Myanmar Crisis', *Reuters*, 12th March 2018. https://reut.rs/3v7gKdQ

21 Specia, Megan & Mozur, Paul, 'A War of Words Puts Facebook at the Center of Myanmar's Rohingya Crisis', *The New York Times,* 27th October 2017. https://nyti.ms/3v2Uvp9

22 Lomas, Natasha, 'UN Says Facebook Is Accelerating Ethnic

Violence in Myanmar', *TechCrunch*, 13th March 2018. https://tcrn.ch/3HQDx5c

23 McPherson, Poppy, 'Facebook says it was "too slow" to fight hate Speech in Myanmar', *Reuters,* 16th August 2018. https://reut.rs/3hDwSjV

24 Lomas, Natasha, 'Meta Urged to Pay Reparations for Facebook's Role in Rohingya Genocide'. *TechCrunch*, 29th September 2022. https://tcrn.ch/3WcBoVL

25 Goldfarb, Jeffrey, 'Zuckerberg motivates supervoting stock resistance', *Reuters*, 27th October 2022. https://reut.rs/3PEIPT4

26 Al Jazeera, 'Explainer: How Elon Musk financed his $44bn Twitter takeover', *Al Jazeera,* 28th October 2022. https://bit.ly/3WaEjyj

27 Hatmaker, Taylor, 'Elon Musk just axed key Twitter teams like human rights, accessibility, AI ethics and curation', *TechCrunch,* 4th November 2022. https://tcrn.ch/3FHjy6b

28 Kay, Grace, 'Elon Musk fired 3 Twitter employees that criticized him on social media', *Business Insider,* 15th November 2022. https://bit.ly/3BOpklg

29 Okumoko, Joy, 'What Elon Musk's Twitter Amnesty for Suspended Accounts Means', *MakeUseOf,* 6th December 2022. https://bit.ly/3Wtogew

30 Rubin, Olivia, Faulders, Katherine, & Steakin, Will, 'Jan. 6 committee condemns Trump as 'central cause' of insurrection in sweeping report', *ABC News,* 19th December 2022. https://abcn.ws/3Wsv7Wd

31 Frenkel, Sheera & Conger, Kate, 'Hate Speech's Rise on Twitter is Unprecedented, Researchers Find', *The New York Times,* 2nd December 2022. https://nyti.ms/3HQLHum

32 Horowitz, Julia & Fung, Brian, "There are red lines': Elon Musk faces international outcry after Twitter bans journalists', *CNN,* 16th December 2022. https://cnn.it/3FAJvUM

33 Zilber, Ariel, 'Jet-tracking teen lashes out at Elon Musk for suspending Twitter account', *The New York Post,* 14th

December 2022. https://bit.ly/3WbNSwP

34 Horowitz, Julia & Fung, Brian, "There are red lines': Elon Musk faces international outcry after Twitter bans journalists', *CNN,* 16th December 2022. https://cnn.it/3FAJvUM

35 Race, Michael, & Kleinman, Zoe, 'Elon Musk: Twitter users vote in favour of boss resigning', *BBC News*, 19th December 2022. https://bbc.in/3HQ2JJ5

36 Kang, Cecilia & Sheera Frenkel, "PizzaGate' Conspiracy Theory Thrives Anew in the TikTok Era', *The New York Times*, 27th June 2020. https://nyti.ms/367WU6I

37 Jensen, Tom, 'Trump Remains Unpopular; Voters Prefer Obama on SCOTUS Pick', *Public Policy Polling* [online], 9th December 2016 (accessed: 25/09/20), https://bit.ly/3mSA09u.

38 Kang, Cecilia & Sheera Frenkel, "PizzaGate' Conspiracy Theory Thrives Anew in the TikTok Era', *The New York Times*, 27th June 2020. https://nyti.ms/367WU6I

39 Kleinman, Zoe, 'Fake news 'travels faster', study finds', *BBC* [online], 9th March 2018 (accessed: 25/09/20), https://bbc.in/3ctAbDt

40 Miller, Zeke, Jill Colvin & Amanda Seitz, 'Trump praised the supporters of QAnon, a conspiracy theory the FBI says is a domestic terrorism threat', *Chicago Tribune*, 19th August 2020. https://bit.ly/3cvwLQm

41 Spring, Marianna & Mike Wendling, 'How Covid-19 myths are merging with the QAnon conspiracy theory', *BBC* [online], 2nd September 2020 (accessed: 09/10/20), https://bbc.in/33IICYH

42 Zuboff, Shoshana, *The Age of Surveillance Capitalism* (London: Profile Books, 2019), p. 161.

43 Zuboff, Shoshana, *The Age of Surveillance Capitalism* (London: Profile Books, 2019), pp. 292-295.

44 Kramer, Adam D. I. , Jamie E. Guillory, and Jeffrey T. Hancock, 'Experimental evidence of massive-scale emotional contagion through social networks', Proceedings of the National

Academy of Sciences of the United States of America, June 2014, 111 (24). https://bit.ly/3k4JFYT

45 'Emotions manipulated in Facebook study', NHS, 1st of July 2014. https://bit.ly/341yEle

46 Isaac, Mike and Cecilia Kang, 'Facebook Says It Won't Back Down From Allowing Lies in Political Ads', *The New York Times*, 9th of January 2020. https://nyti.ms/3j6J9YV

47 Reality Check team, 'Social media: How do other governments regulate it?', *BBC* [online], 12th February 2020 (accessed: 29/09/20), https://bbc.in/2Sb21uU

48 Lepore, Jill, 'How the Simulmatics Corporation Invented the Future', *The New Yorker*, 27th July 2020. https://bit.ly/2HqOjBZ

49 Silber, Tony, 'Big Ideas For A Magazine Newsstand Industry In Distress', *Forbes*, 29th May 2018. https://bit.ly/3n7xsEm

50 Ferguson, Donna, 'How supermarkets get your data – and what they do with it', *The Guardian*, 8th June 2013. https://bit.ly/3hVA8RV

51 Green, Adam, 'Facebook's 52,000 data points on each person reveal something shocking about its future', *Komando* [online], 17th September 2018 (accessed: 23/09/20), https://bit.ly/2FJmpAL

52 Phillips, Toby, 'Facebook's 'FarmVille' a Big Hit with Gamers', ABC News [online], 4th November 2009 (accessed: 23/09/20), https://abcn.ws/3cp5cZ3

53 Bell, Erin, 'Zynga's Bill Mooney on FarmVille: 83 million monthly users and counting', *GameZebo* [online], 16th March 2010 (accessed: 23/09/20), https://bit.ly/361JQ2O

54 Griffiths, Mark D., 'Games introduce children to principles of gambling', *The Independent*, 3rd February 2013. https://bit.ly/3cRQcDv

55 Anonymous, 'Zynga - Contract Information', internet Archive: Wayback Machine [online], 7th January 2009, https://bit.ly/36dlFyH

56 Rosenberg, Matthew, Nicholas Confessore & Carole Cadwalladr, 'How Trump Consultants Exploited the Facebook Data of Millions', *The New York Times*, 17th March 2018. https://nyti.ms/3hRbnGl

57 Anonymous, 'What Is Psychographics? Understanding The Tech That Threatens Elections', *Research Briefs*, 6th May 2020 (accessed 23/09/20), https://bit.ly/32X3X0h

58 Hindman, Matthew, 'How Cambridge Analytica's Facebook targeting model really worked – according to the person who built it', *The Conversation* [online], 30th March 2018 (accessed 29/09/20), https://bit.ly/33axvY8

59 Santos, Mateus Renno & Alexander Testa, 'Homicide is declining around the world – but why?', *The Conversation* [online], 4th November 2019, (accessed: 23/09/20), https://bit.ly/360oMKb

60 Ashworth, Louis & Todd Gillespie, 'Who is Dr Aleksandr Kogan, the Cambridge academic accused of misusing Facebook data?', *Varsity* [online], 17th March 2018 (accessed: 29/09/20), https://bit.ly/3cEpzBy

61 Glaser, April, 'The Cambridge Analytica Scandal Is What Facebook-Powered Election Cheating Looks Like', *Slate* [online], 17th March 2018 (accessed: 23/09/20), https://bit.ly/2FSyzap

62 Cadwalladr, Carole & Emma Graham-Harrison, 'Revealed: 50 million Facebook profiles harvested for Cambridge Analytica in major data breach', The Guardian, 17th March 2018. https://bit.ly/3j88FO4

63 Green, Adam, 'Facebook's 52,000 data points on each person reveal something shocking about its future', Komando [online], 17th September 2018 (accessed: 23/09/20), https://bit.ly/2FJmpAL

64 Dielert, Johann, & Johnson, Robert, 'Facebook: Average Revenue per User (ARPU)', *The Good Estate*, March 2021. https://bit.ly/3l7b6m8

65 Clement, J., 'Facebook's average revenue per user (ARPU) from 2012 to 2019', *Statista* [online], 3rd February 2020 (accessed: 25/09/20), https://bit.ly/2RY7ipp

66 Cuofano, Gennaro, 'Facebook Ad Revenue', *FourWeekMBA,* 10th November 2022. https://bit.ly/3WeCGQ7

67 Anonymous, 'Why are internet cookies called cookies?', inlife [online], ? (accessed 25/09/20), https://bit.ly/3677WJC

68 Brain, Marshall, 'How internet Cookies Work', *HowStuffWorks* [online], 26th April 2000 (accessed: 11/08/20), https://bit.ly/3lQjZzu

69 Anonymous, 'What is a Cookie File/Folder?', *allaboutcookies* [online], N/A (accessed: 11/08/20), https://bit.ly/3kCCgQS

70 Anon, Denis, 'How cookies track you around the web and how to stop them', *Privacy.net* [online], 24th of February 2018 (accessed: 11/08/20), https://bit.ly/341tG8i

71 Anonymous, 'GDPR in the USA | GDPR compliance in US | GDPR and PII', *Cookiebot* [online], 7th July 2020 (accessed: 25/09/20), https://bit.ly/3nZldKA

72 All the above screenshots were taken at https://www.theguardian.com/uk, accessed from a private browser. Screenshots 1 and 3 were taken on 20/09/20. Screenshot 2 was taken on 01/02/23.

73 Ahern, Pat, '25 Mind-Bottling SEO Stats for 2021 (+ Beyond)', *Junto,* January 4th 2021. https://bit.ly/3cdPY9z

74 StatCounter, 'Search Engine Market Share United States of America', *StatCounter Global Statistics,* February 2021. https://bit.ly/3cb1wui

75 StatCounter, 'Search Engine Market Share United Kingdom', *StatCounter Global Statistics,* February 2021. https://bit.ly/2POiuqX

76 Agrawal, AJ, 'How To Optimize Your SEO Results Through Content Creation', *Forbes,* 30th August 2017. https://bit.ly/3kXgpVb

77 Zuboff, Shoshana, *The Age of Surveillance Capitalism*

(London: Profile Books, 2019), p. 103.

78 Zuboff, Shoshana, *The Age of Surveillance Capitalism* (London: Profile Books, 2019), p. 103.

79 Robinson, Duncan, 'Facebook faces EU fine over WhatsApp data-sharing', *Financial Times*, 20th December 2016.

80 Adams, Tim, 'Margrethe Vestager: 'We are doing this because people are angry'', *The Observer*, 17th of September 2017.

81 Doffman, Zak, 'New WhatsApp And Facebook Encryption 'Backdoors'—What's Really Going On', *Forbes*, 29th September 2019.

82 Lomas, Natasha, 'WhatsApp to share user data with Facebook for ad targeting — here's how to opt out', *TechCrunch* [online], 25th August 2016 (accessed: 13/08/20), https://tcrn.ch/33WBUPe

83 'WhatsApp FAQ - How Do I Choose Not to Share My Account Information with Facebook to Improve My Facebook Ads and Products Experiences?' *WhatsApp.com*, 26th August 2016, https://bit.ly/3dvSbxv

84 Brandom, Russel, 'Shadow profiles are the biggest flaw in Facebook's privacy defense', *The Verge* [online], 11th April 2018 (accessed: 25/09/20), https://bit.ly/2G2KqTf

85 Isaac, Mike, 'Zuckerberg Plans to Integrate WhatsApp, Instagram and Facebook Messenger', *The New York Times*, 25th January 2019. https://nyti.ms/337bVnH

86 Zuboff, Shoshana, *The Age of Surveillance Capitalism* (London: Profile Books, 2019), p. 102.

87 Roose, Kevin, 'The Making of a YouTube Radical', *The New York Times*, 8th June 2019. https://nyti.ms/3nX3zHw

88 Miller, Zeke, Jill Colvin & Amanda Seitz, 'Trump praised the supporters of QAnon, a conspiracy theory the FBI says is a domestic terrorism threat', Chicago Tribune, 19th August 2020. https://bit.ly/3cvwLQm

89 Lomans, Natasha, 'Study of YouTube comments finds

evidence of radicalization effect', TechCrunch [online], 28th January 2020 (accessed: 18/08/20), https://tcrn.ch/352iEPi

90 Narayanan, Vidya et al, 'Polarization, Partisanship and Junk News Consumption over Social Media in the US', *Oxford internet Institute*, 6th February 2018. https://bit.ly/2S8hMCD

91 Tufekci, Zeynep, 'YouTube, the Great Radicalizer', *The New York Times*, 18th March 2018. https://nyti.ms/2HeVXPS

92 Zuboff, Shoshana, The Age of Surveillance Capitalism (London: Profile Books, 2019), p. 23.

93 Shields, Mike, 'Amazon Looms Quietly in Digital Ad Landscape', *The Wall Street Journal*, 6th October 2016. https://on.wsj.com/2FD6Ni4

94 McLaughlin, Kevin, 'Bezos Ordered Alexa App Push', *The Information* [online], 16th November 2016 (accessed: 18/08/20),https://bit.ly/2H8GCjQ

95 Fortune Editors, 'The Exec Behind Amazon's Alexa: Full Transcript of Fortune's Interview', *Fortune* [online], 14th July 2016 (accessed: 28/08/20), https://bit.ly/3j5I17G

96 Zuboff, Shoshana, The Age of Surveillance Capitalism (London: Profile Books, 2019), p. 267.

97 Maheshwari, Sapna, 'Hey, Alexa, What Can You Hear? And What Will You Do With It?' *The New York Times*, 31st March 2018. https://nyti.ms/3lRRTnn

98 Stern, Joanna, 'Facebook Really Is Spying on You, Just Not Through Your Phone's Mic', *The Wall Street Journal*, 7th March 2018. https://on.wsj.com/2Ivpmpm

99 Cox, Joseph, & Cole, Samantha, 'How Hackers Are Breaking Into Ring Cameras', *Vice,* 11th December 2019. https://bit.ly/38lWU3e

100 Day, Matt, Giles Turner, and Natalia Drozdiak, 'Amazon Workers Are Listening to What You Tell Alexa', *Bloomberg* [online], 10th April 2019 (accessed: 29/09/20). https://bloom.bg/3i9UK9f

101 Roettgers, Janko, 'Google's secret home security

superpower: Your smart speaker with its always-on mics', *protocol* [online], 3rd August 2020 (accessed: 29/09/20), https://bit.ly/2G8PGox

102 Shead, Sam, 'Amazon Echo and Google Home owners spied on by apps', *BBC* [online], 21st October 2019 (accessed: 25/09/20), https://bbc.in/3j8igog

103 Bond, Casey, 'Is Your Phone Recording Your Conversations? The Answer Might Surprise You.', *HuffPost* [online], 17th August 2019 (accessed: 29/09/20), https://bit.ly/3iieo2B

104 Nichols, Sam, 'Your Phone Is Listening and it's Not Paranoia', *Vice* [online], 5th June 2018 (accessed 25/09/20), https://bit.ly/2FR88lC

105 Zuboff, Shoshana, 'The Age of Surveillance Capitalism', *PublicAffairs,* 4th October 2018.

106 FaceApp Terms of Use Agreement: https://www.faceapp.com/terms-en.html

107 FaceApp Privacy Policy: https://www.faceapp.com/privacy-en.html

108 Collie, Meghan, "Just walk away from it': The scary things companies like FaceApp can do with your data', *Global News* [online], 19th July 2019 (accessed: 19/08/20), https://bit.ly/3o0jbK8

109 Mannion, Patrick, 'Facial-recognition sensors adapt to track emotions, mood, and stress', *EDN* [online], 3rd March 2016 (accessed: 18/08/20), https://bit.ly/379sq4Z

110 Levin, Sam, 'New AI can guess whether you're gay or straight from a photograph', The Guardian, 8th September 2017. https://bit.ly/3nZnNQM

111 Harwell, Drew, 'Federal study confirms racial bias of many facial-recognition systems, casts doubt on their expanding use', *The Washington Post*, 19th December 2019. https://wapo.st/3df2upG

112 Story, Louise, 'Anywhere the Eye Can See, It's Likely to

See an Ad', *The New York Times*, 15th January 2007. https://nyti.ms/337ojUJ.

113 Eyal, Nir, 'Infinite Scroll: The Web's Slot Machine', Tech Crunch [online], 18th August 2012 (accessed: 25/09/20), https://tcrn.ch/2S0SLJK

114 Weinschenk, Susan, 'The Dopamine Seeking-Reward Loop', *Psychology Today* [online], 28th February 2018 (accessed 29/09/20), https://bit.ly/3jri3gh

115 Benson, Buster, 'You are almost definitely not living in reality because your brain doesn't want you to', *Quartz* [online], 16th September 2016 (accessed 29/09/20), https://bit.ly/34b4bzZ

116 Ofcom (2015), 'Public Service Broadcasting in the internet Age', Ofcom, London. https://bit.ly/3rItkws

117 UK Office of Communications (Ofcom) & Jigsaw Research, 'News Consumption in the UK: 2022', *Ofcom,* 21st July 2022. https://bit.ly/3jbbrqN

118 Tobitt, Charlotte, 'Coronavirus leads to 'staggering demand' for trusted TV news', *Press Gazette* [online], 17th March 2020 (accessed: 30/09/20). https://bit.ly/3jhWO03

119 Desikan, Anita, 'How COVID-19 Disinformation Goes Viral', *Union of Concerned Scientists* [online], 16th July 2020 (accessed 21/08/20). https://bit.ly/2H7YwTM

120 Anonymous, 'COVID-19 Disinformation: How to Spot It—and Stop It', Union of Concerned Scientists [online], 14th July 2020 (accessed: 21/08/21). https://bit.ly/3o0mMI8

121 OECD (2020), 'Combatting COVID-19 disinformation on online platforms', OECD, Paris. https://bit.ly/2FDM1Po

122 Desikan, Anita, 'How COVID-19 Disinformation Goes Viral', *Union of Concerned Scientists* [online], 16th July 2020 (accessed 21/08/20). https://bit.ly/2H7YwTM

123 Marineau, Sophie, 'Russian disinformation in the time of Covid-19', *The Conversation* [online], 8th July 2020 (accessed: 21/08/20), https://bit.ly/37auw4w

124 Brashier, Nadia & Daniel Schacter, 'Older people spread more fake news, a deadly habit in the COVID-19 pandemic', *Los Angeles Times*, 7th August 2020. https://lat.ms/346z3BL

125 Desikan, Anita, 'How COVID-19 Disinformation Goes Viral', *Union of Concerned Scientists* [online], 16th July 2020 (accessed 21/08/20). https://bit.ly/3529Tox

126 Shead, Sam, 'Facebook, Twitter and YouTube pull 'false' coronavirus video after it goes viral', *CNBC* [online], 28th July 2020 (accessed: 29/09/20), https://cnb.cx/34b10IG

127 Queensland University Of Technology, 'COVID-19 / 5G Infodemic: A Perfect Storm for Conspiracy Theories', *SciTechDaily* [online], 8th August 2020 (accessed: 29/09/20), https://bit.ly/33dOqcl

128 Wakefield, Jane, 'How Bill Gates became the voodoo doll of Covid conspiracies', *BBC* [online], 5th June 2020 (accessed 29/09/20), https://bbc.in/3l9Zduz

129 Avaaz (2020), 'Facebook's Algorithm: A Major Threat to Public Health', Avaaz, New York City. https://bit.ly/3jgrZJb

130 Fung, Brian & Ahiza Garcia, 'Facebook has shut down 5.4 billion fake accounts this year', *CNN* [online], 13th November 2019 (accessed: 29/09/20), https://cnn.it/2GeaASR

131 BBC, 'Twitter 'shuts down millions of fake accounts'', *BBC* [online], 9th July 2018 (accessed: 29/09/20), https://bbc.in/3jhAh3I

132 Abrams, Abigail, 'Here's What We Know So Far About Russia's 2016 Meddling', *Time*, 18th April 2019. https://bit.ly/33dpwtC

133 Desiderio, Andrew & Kyle Cheney, 'Democrats see payoff from pressure campaign on intelligence community', *Politico* [online] 8th August 2020 (accessed: 29/09/20). https://politi.co/3cGKggb

134 Intelligence and Security Committee of Parliament (2020), 'Russia', Intelligence and Security Committee of Parliament, London. https://bit.ly/30jKJQx

135 Coppins, McKay, 'The Billion-Dollar Disinformation Campaign to Reelect the President', *The Atlantic,* March 2020. https://bit.ly/3qw9UKb

136 Mac, Ryan, 'Instagram Displayed Negative Related Hashtags For Biden, But Hid Them For Trump', *Buzzfeed* [online], 5th August 2020 (accessed: 29/09/20). https://bit.ly/3la7oaf

137 Schifrin, Nick & Dan Sagalyn, 'How China's high-tech 'eyes' monitor behavior and dissent', *PBS NewsHour* [online], 30th September 2019 (accessed: 29/09/20), https://to.pbs.org/346drWl

138 Ma, Alexandra, 'China has started ranking citizens with a creepy 'social credit' system — here's what you can do wrong, and the embarrassing, demeaning ways they can punish you', *Business Insider* [online], 29th October 2018 (accessed: 29/09/20). https://bit.ly/2S90fKH

139 Booth, Robert, 'Robots to be used in UK care homes to help reduce loneliness', *The Guardian*, 7th September 2020. https://bit.ly/36iB2Wq

140 Everett, Chet, 'UK A-level algorithm fiasco a global example of what not to do - what went wrong and why', *Diginomica* [online], 24th August 2020 (accessed: 29/09/20). https://bit.ly/36g6sg4

141 Human Rights Watch (2020), 'Automated Hardship: How the Tech-Driven Overhaul of the UK's Social Security System Worsens Poverty', Human Rights Watch, New York City. https://bit.ly/3jlPB9y

142 Metz, Rachel, 'Elon Musk hopes to put a computer chip in your brain. Who wants one?', *CNN* [online], 21st July 2019 (accessed: 29/09/20), https://cnn.it/30hJWQa

143 The Economist Editors, 'The world's most valuable resource is no longer oil, but data', *The Economist Online*, 6th May 2017, (accessed 9 October 2020), https://econ.st/30PRc5Z

144 Lohr, Steve, 'He Created the Web. Now He's Out to

Remake the Digital World', *The New York Times,* 10th January 2021, (accessed 12 February 2021). https://nyti.ms/3rZi8v9

145 Fung, Brian & Ahiza Garcia, 'Facebook has shut down 5.4 billion fake accounts this year', *CNN* [online], 13th November 2019 (accessed: 29/09/20), https://cnn.it/2GeaASR

146 Fair Vote UK (2020), 'Defending our Democracy in the Digital Age', Fair Vote UK, London. https://bit.ly/3l3r4fT

147 Fair Vote UK (2020), 'Defending our Democracy in the Digital Age', Fair Vote UK, London. https://bit.ly/3l3r4fT

148 Knowledge@Wharton, 'What's Fueling the Smart City Backlash?', *Wharton, University of Pennsylvania,* 24th September 2019. https://whr.tn/3br41tk

149 Lochhead, Colton, 'Bill would allow tech companies to create local governments', *Las Vegas Review Journal,* 3rd February 2021, (accessed 12 February 2021), https://bit.ly/3tY5myZ

150 Smith, Ben, 'Trump Wants Back on Facebook. This Star-Studded Jury Might Let Him', *The New York Times,* 24th January 2021. https://nyti.ms/2OGkHnK

151 Scott, Mark, Larger, Thibault & Kiyali, Laura, 'Europe rewrites rulebook for digital age', *Politico*, 15th December 2020, https://politi.co/3CcMNwX

152 Hern, Alex, 'Government criticised over renewed delay to online safety bill', *The Guardian*, 27th October 2022. https://bit.ly/3WdB88Y

153 Milmo, Dan, 'Lawsuit aiming to break up Facebook group Meta can go ahead, US court rules', *The Guardian*, 12th January 2022. https://bit.ly/3Wtghy6

BOOK CLUB DISCUSSION GUIDE

—

First, did you enjoy the Little Black Book of Social Media? Let us know on Twitter (the irony!):

Kyle is @kyletaylor

Byline Books is @BylineTimes

Second, do you want to discuss it with friends and family but they need to read it first? The book will always be available at littleblackdatabook.com

Third, here are some questions to get conversation started:

❖ What was your initial reaction to the book? Shock? Disbelief? "I told you so?"

❖ The book gives several examples of conspiracy theories that took hold on social media. Have you or has someone you know ever – knowingly or unknowingly gotten wrapped up in one? How did it happen? What did you do?

❖ Is social media addictive? How does it make you feel to think about never using Facebook, Instagram, Twitter, TikTok or Snapchat again?

❖ The idea that we may be living in a post-truth
  world is a central theme to the book. Do you
  agree? If so, do you think we can find our way
  back as a society? How?

❖ There is an entire section on what you can do
  to protect your privacy and data, fix democracy
  and save the world. What actions do you plan
  to take? When? Remember, there is no time like
  the present!

ABOUT THE AUTHOR

Kyle Taylor is the creator of the "Little Black Book" series. This book was originally published as "The Little Black Book of Data and Democracy" in March 2021 and has been updated and republished as "The Little Black Book of Social Media" to ensure it remains on the cutting edge of these important issues.

Kyle is the founder of Fair Vote UK, which published whistleblower evidence of Vote Leave's lawbreaking in the EU referendum and supported Chris Wylie's whistleblower revelations around Cambridge Analytica's global data theft and misappropriation. He is a leading campaigner on digital democracy reform and platform regulation. He has has spent the last half-decade working to hold lying politicians like Boris Johnson to account, which inspired The Little Black Book of Lying Boris Johnson, published in December 2022.

Kyle was the Campaign Director and Chief of Staff to a UK government minister and has worked on half a dozen election campaigns in the UK and the USA, including the 2016 US Presidential Campaign and the 2020 US Georgia Senate Runoff. He is a graduate of American University and the London School of Economics and a Peace Centre Fellow in Tokyo, Japan where his work is focussed on disinformation and the erosion of democracy. This is his fourth book and the third in the Little Black Book series.